VICKI COBB

SEE FOR YOURSELF

MORE THAN 100

EXPERIMENTS

FOR SCIENCE FAIRS

AND PROJECTS

Illustrated by Dave Klug

SCHOLASTIC REFERENCE

For my grandchildren: Abby, Lexie, Ben, Jonathan, and Jillian

ACKNOWLEDGMENTS

The author gratefully acknowledges the help of the following people: Dr. Marcia Pelchat, Monell Chemical Senses Center; David Landrigan for the blob figures; Dr. Matthew M. Botvinick for the Real Rubber Arm illusion; Dr. Barry Green of The John B. Pierce Laboratory, Yale University for the Cold Fooler experiment; Dr. Eric H. Chudler of the University of Washington for the sidedness experiment; Mike Swift of Whirley Industries; The American Chemical Society for the Vegetable Dye procedure that appeared in Vol. 5, May 1991; consummate science teacher Ed Escudero of Summit County School for sources and science procedures too numerous to mention. A special thanks to my game assistant, Ned Stuart, who was always ready to experiment; to my marvelously enthusiastic editor, Kate Waters, for her attention to detail and buoyant support; and to my husband, Richard Trachtenberg, who nods silently to my constant enthusing over science experiments.

Art on page 29 adapted with permission from *The Best of Science*, The American Chemical Society, 1997.

Some of the material in this book has been previously published.

LIBRARY OF CONGRESS CATALOGING-IN-PUBLICATION DATA

Cobb, Vicki. · See for yourself: more than 100 experiments for science fairs and projects / by Vicki Cobb; illustrated by Dave Klug. p. cm. · Includes index. · 1. Science projects—Juvenile literature. 2. Science—Experiments—Juvenile literature. [Science—Experiments. 2. Experiments. 3. Science projects.] I. Klug, Dave, ill. II. Title. · Q182.3 .C62 2001 · 507′.8—dc21 · 00-044579 · ISBN 0-439-09010-5 (pob); ISBN 0-439-09011-3 (pb)

10 9 8 7 6 5 4 3 2 1   01 02 03 04
Printed in the U.S.A.   23

First printing, September 2001

Expert reader: Paul Vetter, Staff Scientist,
E.O. Lawrence Berkeley National Laboratory, Berkeley, California
Art direction: Nancy Sabato · Book design: Kay Petronio · Composition: Barbara Balch
Illustrations: Dave Klug · Cover design: Kristen Ekeland

Contents

Why Science Anyhow?

If you relied only on your senses to learn about the world you live in, you might get some wrong ideas. You might guess that the earth is flat, or that heavy objects fall to the earth faster than light ones. You would want to make sense of your world, so you might invent a god driving a chariot across the sky to explain how the sun rises and sets. To explain why popcorn pops, you might imagine a tiny demon inside a kernel of unpopped popcorn, who throws a temper tantrum and explodes when his house is heated. Today's technology would seem impossible, even magical, to you.

What has made the difference? The answer is science. Without science we would be living much as people did thousands of years ago. Before that we had centuries of trial and error. People learned how to grow food, use herbs, and build structures without truly understanding why their discoveries worked. Modern science is a relatively new approach to learning about the world (although there were individuals who thought scientifically thousands of years ago).

Scientists do experiments—systematic and carefully controlled trials—to discover the relationships between causes and effects. Methods and results are shared so that others may try experiments and see for themselves. Scientific knowledge comes bit by bit, as each experiment becomes a piece of a larger and larger puzzle. Eventually, we know enough to apply the knowledge in unique ways, and, Ta da! a new technology is possible. The world will never be the same.

This book is your opportunity to find out how it feels to be a scientist. Science begins in a small way—you look around and ask a question about something specific in your environment. The best questions suggest a way to find the answer: "What would happen if . . .?" or "How is ___ related to ____?" or "Will it still work if I change ___?" There is nothing quite like the feeling of wondering about something, designing an experiment to shed light on it, and actually making a discovery.

Archimedes, who lived in Egypt more than two thousand years ago, was one of the first to think scientifically. He had to figure out if the gold in a king's crown was pure. To do this, he needed to measure its volume and its weight. But how could he measure the volume without melting it down? The answer came to him as he lowered himself into the bathtub and noticed that the water level rose. He figured that the volume of water displaced was equal to the volume of his body and that water displacement could be used to measure the volume of the king's crown. "Eureka!" (Greek for "I've got it!") he shouted and went leaping out the door so enthralled with his insight that he forgot to put his clothes on. I don't expect you to get this carried away, but I hope that you will have many small "eurekas!" in your own way.

At the beginning of this introduction I said that you can't always depend on your senses. You might say to me, "How do you know?" As a scientist I say to you, "If you do what I did, then you will know what I know. I can show you lots of ways that your senses can be fooled." Science is a way of replicating another person's experience. So, you never have to take anyone's word for something. *You can do an experiment and see for yourself.* You can do experiments with your own senses and other people's to find out just how limited we all are and how we can make mistakes.

And speaking of mistakes, here's something else that's really special about science. Unlike the tests you may take in school, mistakes in science don't matter! What is important is that you learn something. You can often learn just as much from a mistake as you can from getting the correct answer or the answer you expect. Some of the greatest discoveries of all times were mistakes. Penicillin, heat from microwaves, and radioactivity would not have been discovered without mistakes. Finding out that you've been fooled or mistaken can be the beginning of an adventure.

The subject matter of this book is the world in which you live. It begins with you and it takes inspirations from some very familiar places—the supermarket, toy store, hardware store, stationery store, and drugstore. You can get a kick from looking at parts of your life that you take for granted in a completely new and different way.

Science is full of surprises! What happens when you spin a Ping-Pong® ball with ice in it or try and grow yeast in dandruff shampoo? You can make ink from tea and iron pills, extract DNA from onions in your kitchen, and make paper from lint from your dryer. And if you want to enter a science fair, this book is a great place to start.

How to Use This Book

Begin by browsing. Think about the things that interest you. I've grouped experiments together by topics. Several experiments around a single topic can be grouped to be a substantial project. I've left a lot of things open-ended. Mostly I've tried to give you lots of procedures—methods of investigation—that can lead to in-depth studies.

Each experiment also has a challenge level. Quick and easy experiments are rated low on the scale next to the name of the experiment. Particularly challenging experiments are rated high. Most are in the middle range.

Materials for each procedure are listed in the order they are to be used. The "Observations and Suggestions" sections may contain my results from the experiment as well as other activities that may require additional materials. If you need to find an experiment for a particular discipline, or kind of science, look at the Index by Discipline. I've listed experiments in the following subject areas: the human body, life sciences, chemistry and earth science, physical science, and technology.

If you are planning to enter a science fair, there should be several stages to your project. First, give yourself plenty of time. Start thinking about what you want to do as soon as possible, not at the last minute. Pick an area that interests you. Make some notes about what you already know about the subject. Do a procedure from this book. See what ideas you get. Don't be afraid to experiment and fail. If you want to learn more about your experiment, I've listed key words for Internet research at the bottom of each experiment. Type a key word or phrase into a search engine. Some of the information may be extremely technical, but there may be some articles that give you even more ideas.

A word about safety. Use common sense! Don't eat or drink or inhale anything in these projects unless you know that it is a food. Have an adult present when you use the stove or matches, or are dealing with household chemicals.

After you've made some discoveries, think about how to communicate what you've learned with other people. Your exhibit should answer the following questions:

1. Why did the subject of the project interest you? What do most people already know about it? How does it affect your daily life?

2. What questions did you ask about the subject? If there is an outcome to an experiment, what are the things that affect the outcome?

3. How was your experiment designed to answer your question? Give a detailed description of your procedure. It is very important to explain exactly what you did.

4. What are the results of your experiment? How did they answer your questions?

5. What is the significance of the result? What other experiments does your result suggest? How could you apply your discoveries to a technology? What doors do they open?

Be inventive in how you display your project. If possible, set up a learning station so that fair-goers can see for themselves what happens. Use photography, computer graphics, and plenty of color. Be prepared to answer questions about your project. You'll be surprised at how much you know because you have done the procedures. The best way to learn anything is by doing something, not just sitting in an armchair and thinking about it.

And now, let's begin.

CHAPTER 1

Yourself and Other Humans

Y ou and your friends are fascinating subjects for scientists. Human beings are the most complicated of all living things with the most highly developed nervous systems, including our amazing brains. How we get information about the world we live in, how we process that information, and how we respond to it makes us who we are. But if we are so complicated, how can we gain understanding of how we tick?

Fortunately for scientists, we have weaknesses. Our senses are limited and can be fooled. Illusions are clues that can reveal ways your nervous system works. It's fun and enlightening to test the limits of your perceptions. You've got plenty. In this chapter you'll discover some peculiarly odd and interesting things about yourself and your friends. Get ready for some amazing yet humbling experiences.

CHALLENGE LEVEL

THE TRIANGLE TEST

- scissors
- coffee filter paper
- ruler
- sharp knife
- lemon
- lime
- spoon
- pencil
- a blindfolded friend without a cold

Do you have a talented nose? Can you tell the difference between two closely related smells? Can you remember what you smell? The "triangle test" is given to job applicants in the perfume and fragrance industry to see how well they smell. Test yourself and your friends.

Method of Investigation

1 Cut the coffee filter paper into strips about ¼ inch wide and 3 inches long. You need three strips for each test. That's why it's called the "triangle" test.

2 Transfer the oils, which contain the molecules you smell, from the citrus fruit to the end of the test strips. To do this, cut a piece of lemon peel and a piece of lime peel. Place the peel, outside skin side down, on the end of a strip of filter paper. Press the peel over the strip with the back of a spoon to squeeze its oil onto the filter paper. Make one lemon oil strip, one lime oil strip, and either one for the third strip.

Number the ends of the strips so you know which is which.

3 Tell a blindfolded friend that you are going to present three smells and to tell you which two are alike. As you hold a strip under your friend's nose, state the number. Do three trials for the test, alternating the order in which you present the strips. To refresh the nose between sniffs, have your friend sniff a tissue or a sleeve.

Observations & Suggestions

Have your friend try the triangle test on you. Do the triangle test on lots of people. Are females more talented smellers than males? Are adults better smellers than children? Test two brands of coffee, two different perfumes, apricots and nectarines, almond extract and cherry extract, or the cooking water of broccoli and cauliflower.

Key Words: olfaction • sense of smell

YOUR INTERNAL SENSE OF TOUCH

Meeting Fingertips (pg. 11) • Mirror Writing (pg. 12) • Do You Want to Be a Helicopter Pilot? (pg. 12) • Zeroing In (pg. 13)

Close your eyes and imagine the position of your body at this moment. You know where your legs and arms and hands are. You know if you are sitting or standing. Your ability to sense your body and its motions is called *proprioception.* Talented athletes and dancers have a heightened proprioceptive sense. Learning to dance, to type, or to play a musical instrument or a sport, for example, involves practice. Repeated motions train your proprioceptive nerves so that eventually you have a muscle "memory." You can repeat the motion without thinking about it.

Here are some simple activities that investigate your proprioceptive sense.

MEETING FINGERTIPS

CHALLENGE LEVEL

MATERIALS AND EQUIPMENT

● 2 pencils

How good are you at touching your index fingers together? Here are a few tests that make a challenge out of a no-brainer.

Method of Investigation

1 Stand up and extend your arms sideways. Rotate your extended arms from your shoulders three times. Now close your eyes and try to get your fingertips to meet without going past each other.

2 With your eyes open, try this again using pencils pointing directly at each other. Are you more or less accurate with the pencil points than with your fingers? Try again, this time keeping one eye closed. Then try with both eyes closed.

3 Close your eyes and raise both hands over your head. Keep your left hand perfectly still. Touch the tip of your nose with the index fingertip of your right hand. Quickly try and touch the thumb of your left hand (which is still over your head) with your right index fingertip. Try this motion several times, first touching your nose and then attempting to touch your left thumb.

Observations & Suggestions

Do you improve with practice? Does it make a difference when you switch hands? What happens when you wiggle your fingers? Does wiggling help your proprioceptive sense to locate your thumb in space?

Key Words: kinesthesis • proprioception

MIRROR WRITING

CHALLENGE LEVEL

MATERIALS AND EQUIPMENT

- paper
- pencil
- light
- mirror

Can you write backward? Try writing a sentence while looking at your writing hand in a mirror. This is nearly impossible because vision dominates your proprioceptive sense. Moving your hand from left to right is difficult because you're seeing it in reverse in the mirror.

Method of Investigation

You can actually fool your proprioceptive sense into doing mirror writing. Place a half sheet of paper on your forehead. Hold it in place with your nonwriting hand. Holding a pencil with your other hand, place the point on the left side of your forehead. Then write your name or a word such as *hello* in cursive script going from left to right across your forehead. Imagine the page is in front of you and that you are writing normally. Don't think too hard about what you're doing. When you look at what you've written, it appears illegible. But if you look at it in a mirror, or if you turn the paper over and hold it up to the light, it can be easily read.

Key Words: mirror writing · proprioception

DO YOU WANT TO BE A HELICOPTER PILOT?

CHALLENGE LEVEL

MATERIALS AND EQUIPMENT

- several friends

How good is your sense of balance? Helicopter pilots must have a great sense of balance because instruments alone will not keep a helicopter oriented properly in the air. Aspiring helicopter pilots must pass a test of balance. Not many people can do this, perhaps one in twenty. Test yourself and your friends:

Method of Investigation

Stand at attention. Make two fists and extend your arms straight down by your sides. Close your eyes. Bend one leg back at the knee so your lower leg is parallel to the floor and you are standing on one foot. Keep your eyes closed and hold this position for ninety seconds.

Key Words: proprioception · sense of balance

ZEROING IN

MATERIALS AND EQUIPMENT

- pencil or pen
- paper

I f you were blind, how quickly would you learn to feel your way around? Would it be easier to do some things than others? Here are some tests to help you find out.

Method of Investigation

1. Make a zero about ½ inch in diameter on a sheet of paper that is lying on a tabletop. Raise your pen or pencil above your head, close your eyes and make a dot on the paper as close as possible to the center of the zero. How close did you zero in on the zero? Try again. Any better luck? Now try with your eyes open.

2. On a lined sheet of paper, sign your name. Place your pen or pencil after the signature on the same line, close your eyes, and sign your name again. Try writing other words. Can you tell the difference between what you wrote with your eyes closed and what you wrote with your eyes open?

 Most people find that looking at the zero between trials improves their performance. Practice also improves performance. Vision seems to be essential for real accuracy. However, vision is not necessary for reproducing written words. We are used to the "feel" of writing from the proprioceptors in our hands and fingers.

Key Words: proprioception · hand-eye coordination

CHALLENGE LEVEL

THIRD-HAND LEARNING

MATERIALS AND EQUIPMENT

Y ou know your body and its parts. Do you think you can be fooled into feeling as if a fake rubber hand belongs to you?

Method of Investigation

1 Have your subject sit facing you at a table. Since I obtained a rubber right hand, my subject had his right arm on the table with his palm up. If you get a left hand, your subject's left arm should rest on the table.

2 Position the barrier so that your subject's arm and hand are out of the sight of your subject. Place the rubber hand in front of your subject with the palm up. Drape the plastic bag over the barrier and the wrist of the rubber hand.

3 Hold a paintbrush in each hand. Instruct your subject to watch the rubber hand. Simultaneously stroke both the rubber hand and the subject's hand. Keep it up for about five minutes. Afterward, give your subject the questionnaire in the box on page 15.

- a friend
- a table
- a life-sized rubber model of a human hand (you can get one from a party store around Halloween or from a costume specialty shop at other times of the year)
- some kind of screen or barrier—a big piece of oak tag or a pile of books works well—so that your subject cannot see his or her own hand when resting on a table.
- a large black trash bag
- 2 identical small paintbrushes
- timer (optional)

Observations & Suggestions

This illusion is really about where the subject feels the touch is occurring. The subject's sense of the location of his or her real hand is distorted so that she feels as if her real hand is closer to the rubber hand than it actually is. You can check this out with another experiment. Both before and after the experiment, ask your subject to close her eyes

There are two types of receptor cells in the skin. One type is simply a free nerve ending. Scientists believe that these cells are responsible for feeling pain. The other type has a cell body close to the nerve end. These have been associated with feeling pressure and temperature and sometimes with pain. All of the nerves send messages to the brain, which interprets the messages. This interpretation is called perception.

QUESTIONNAIRE

Rate your answer from 1 to 6 where **6 means you agree strongly** and **1 means you disagree strongly**.

During the experiment there were times when:

_____ It seemed as if I were feeling the touch of the paintbrush in the location where I saw the rubber hand touched.

_____ It seemed as though the touch I felt was caused by the paintbrush touching the rubber hand.

_____ I felt as if the rubber hand were my hand.

---

and line up her index finger that is under the table with her index finger that is resting on the table. You may find that your subject's finger is closer to the rubber hand after the illusion than it was before.

You will also find that some people experience the illusion more quickly than others. The majority of those who experience the illusion feel the touch of the brush on the rubber hand that they're watching, not on their own hand that's hidden from them. The brain adjusts by assuming that the subject's real hand is in the position of the rubber hand. Weird!

TEMPERATURE ILLUSIONS

Hot or Cold? (pg. 16) · Cool Fooler (pg. 17) · A Very Hot Illusion (pg. 18)

One of the jobs of your skin is to maintain a constant body temperature of 98.6°F. When you feel neutral—neither warm nor cold—you are not aware of temperature. Keeping comfortable depends on your skin being able to sense a temperature change.

CHALLENGE LEVEL

HOT OR COLD?

MATERIALS AND EQUIPMENT

3 large bowls of water:
- 1 bowl of cold water
- 1 bowl of very warm water (not too hot to touch)
- 1 bowl of water at room temperature

How can the temperature of a bowl of water be both warm and cool? It depends on where you're coming from.

Method of Investigation

Place one hand in the cold water and one in the very warm water until you are no longer aware of the coldness or warmth of the water. This may take several minutes. Then plunge both hands into the water at room temperature.

Observations & Suggestions

The first stage of the experiment lets your heat and cold receptors adapt to the temperature of the water. Adaptation means that you are no longer sensitive to a temperature that at first felt warm or cold. That's why you can swim in cool water and you can soak in a very hot tub.

The water at room temperature will feel cool to the hand that's been in hot water and warm to the hand that's been in cold water. That's because the sensation of warmth or coldness is determined largely by the temperature to which the skin has adapted before the hands are plunged into the same room-temperature water.

Key Words: temperature perception · touch and illusion

COOL FOOLER

- 3 pennies
- a refrigerator

Which is more accurate: your ability to sense temperature or your ability to sense pressure? The next illusion is one answer to this question.

Method of Investigation

1 Put two pennies in the refrigerator for about five minutes.

2 Hold the third penny for the same amount of time so that it becomes the temperature of your hand.

3 Quickly place the two pennies from the refrigerator on a counter in a line with the "neutral" penny in the middle. Place the first three fingers of one hand on each of the three pennies. What temperature is perceived by the middle finger?

Observations & Suggestions

Amazingly, all three pennies feel cold, including the one in the middle. This is because your sense of pressure is more accurate than your temperature sense. Your brain assumes that a temperature stimulation that comes from the same place as a pressure stimulation is caused by the pressure stimulation. Since there is pressure on all three fingers, the middle finger is fooled into feeling cold, just like the two outer fingers, although the penny is the same temperature as the finger.

Do you get the same effect when the two outer pennies have been warmed up by putting them in hot water and the middle penny is neutral?

Your skin has receptor cells that are sensitive to either hot or cold but not to both. The heat receptors respond to warmth with an increase in the number of messages sent to the brain, or *firing rate*. They react when the temperature is between 73°F and 117°F with the most nerves firing at 100°F, just above body temperature. Above 117°F they stop reacting, and heat-sensitive pain receptors begin to fire. Cold receptors fire as the skin gets cooler between the temperatures of about 95°F and 55°F. (Remember, the skin is only a few degrees cooler than the interior body temperature of 98.6°F.) The largest amount of firing occurs around 77°F. They also fire when things get very hot from 113°F to 122°F. At higher temperatures, the receptors are too damaged to fire.

Key Words: touch and illusion · touch receptors

A VERY HOT ILLUSION

CHALLENGE LEVEL

MATERIALS AND EQUIPMENT

- 2 1-foot-long pipe cleaners (known as chenille stems in craft stores)
- 2 small bowls
- hot and cold water

What happens when very warm and cool temperature stimulation are close to each other in a way you don't normally experience?

Method of Investigation

1. Lay the pipe cleaners flat and bend them back and forth so that they look like an S. Nest the pipe cleaners together and put them on the counter.

2. Fill one bowl with cold tap water and the other with very warm but not overly hot tap water. Put a pipe cleaner in each bowl.

3. Working quickly, remove the pipe cleaners and fit them together again on the counter. Put your forearm gently on top of the pipe cleaners. Surprise! The sensation is not what you'd expect!

Observations & Suggestions

Instead of feeling warm, or warm and cool, the combined stimulation produces a feeling of intense heat. Some people find it so hot that they have to remove their arm from the pipe cleaners. The temperatures of the pipe cleaners stimulate both cold and warm receptors in the same area of the arm. In this case, the brain interprets this as a single, very hot sensation.

18

Key Words: touch illusions • temperature and perception

THE STROOP EFFECT: MEMORY VS. COLOR PERCEPTION

CHALLENGE LEVEL

MATERIALS AND EQUIPMENT

- white paper
- a set of colored marking pens
- a stopwatch

What happens when two activities compete for attention in your brain? J. R. Stroop, an English psychologist, made an interesting discovery in 1935. You can, too.

Method of Investigation

1. On a sheet of white paper, write the first list of words in the color indicated in the parentheses.

2. On another sheet of white paper, write the second list of meaningless words in the color indicated in the parentheses.

3. Using the first sheet of words, ask a friend to name the *colors* of the words, not what the words say, as quickly as possible. Time the test with a stopwatch.

4. Ask your friend to name the colors of the meaningless words. Time the test. Which test was faster?

Observations & Suggestions

In the first example, you will find that most people can't ignore the words. Their ability to read is so ingrained in their memory that it is difficult to suppress the urge to read and just name the color without making an extra effort. Stroop demonstrated that it takes longer to name the color when the words are the names of colors than when the words have nothing to do with color. In this case, there is a mental competition between the normal response to a written word—reading—and the one required by the test—naming the color of the letters.

What happens when you try the test using color-related words like sky, rose, grass, sun, pumpkin, written in random colors? Are the results different than when you used words that are names of colors or nonsense words?

List 1

red (red)	**blue** (blue)	**orange** (orange)	**purple** (purple)
orange (orange)	**blue** (blue)	**green** (green)	**red** (red)
blue (green)	**purple** (red)	**green** (purple)	**red** (blue)
orange (blue)	**blue** (red)	**red** (green)	**blue** (purple)
green (orange)	**red** (blue)	**blue** (purple)	**purple** (green)
orange (purple)	**blue** (green)	**red** (orange)	**green** (red)

List 2

ngfy (red)	**xbts** (blue)	**ndhire** (orange)	**cnhdes** (purple)
mhedyh (orange)	**bhfe** (blue)	**pjeyl** (green)	**njf** (red)
fsbfkv (blue)	**lgbf** (red)	**fwa** (green)	**zjdcv** (orange)
nglkcd (red)	**vyhfrd** (green)	**cft** (orange)	**mkgl** (purple)
lxndyf (orange)	**hou** (blue)	**mlcg** (purple)	**noudgt** (green)
olftcs (purple)	**frjs** (green)	**lvd** (orange)	**uhths** (red)

Key Words: Stroop effect · color perception

A VISION OF VISION

Vision is the dominant sense in human beings. You have more nerve receptors in your eyes than in all your other senses combined. You are also more susceptible to visual illusions than to illusions in your other senses. There are many books of optical illusions. Here are a few less well known illusions that shed some light on the way you see.

DISCOVER YOUR BLIND SPOT

CHALLENGE LEVEL

MATERIALS AND EQUIPMENT

- clown diagram (see below)
- tape measure
- calculator

Do you know where your blind spot is? Everyone's got two—one in each eye! You can easily discover where yours are located.

Method of Investigation

Close one eye and look steadily at the X between the two clowns. Don't shift your gaze to either clown. Move the page forward and back. The clown on the right will disappear when you look with your right eye and the left clown will disappear when you look with your left eye.

Observations & Suggestions

Scientists locate the blind spot by measuring the angle of your line of sight. You can measure it, too. Have a friend measure the distance between your eye and the X when the page is the right distance away from your face for the clown to be in your blind spot. Now you can make a calculation that will let you compare the angle of your blind spot with those of other people.

You know the distance between your eye and the X, and you know the distance between the X and the clown. The angle between these two measurements is a right angle of 90°. A triangle with a right angle in it is called a

 ———————— X ————————

right triangle. You can find the angle in a right triangle if you know the lengths of the sides by using the formula for the *tangent* of the angle. All you have to do is divide the side opposite the mystery angle (the one nearest the eye) by the side adjacent to the mystery angle.

In other words, the length of the distance from X to the clown is divided by the distance from the eye to the X.

The formula is:

$$\frac{\text{Distance from X to clown}}{\text{Distance from eye to X}} = \text{tangent of the angle}$$

If you do this on a calculator, you will end up with a number that can be carried to four decimal places. This is the tangent. To find your mystery angle (in degrees), you just find the angle whose tangent is equal to the number you calculated. Many calculators will do this for you. (Since there are many ways of doing this on a calculator, ask someone who's familiar with your particular calculator to help you.) You can also look for your angle on trigonometry tables of tangent.

Once you have a measurement for the angle of vision for your blind spot, you can see if other people have the same angle or different angles. Are all human eyeballs pretty much alike? You have to do research to find out.

Light enters the eye through the pupil, a hole in the iris—the colored part of the eye (see the diagram on page 25). Just behind the pupil is the lens, which focuses the image onto the retina, a circular area at the back of the eyeball that is full of blood vessels and light receptor cells. The receptor cells fire in a pattern, which depends on the image, and send a message to the brain through the optic nerve. The only part of the retina that doesn't contain any receptors is the place where the optic nerve attaches to the eyeball. This is your blind spot. Notice that your blind spot is not in the middle of your line of sight, but off to one side.

Key Words: sense of sight · blind spot · optic nerve

CHALLENGE LEVEL

FILLING-IN ILLUSIONS

MATERIALS AND EQUIPMENT

- red pen
- fixation point boxes (see below)
- sheet of white paper

Do you see everything you look at? Can your brain edit out some of what you see? Do this test to find out.

Method of Investigation

1 Use a red pen to color in the two white squares in each figure.

2 Cover Figure 2 and Figure 3 with a sheet of white paper.

3 Stare at the small red block in the corner marked fixation point in Figure 1. Hold your gaze as steady as possible.

After ten or fifteen seconds, the larger red square in the center should start to fade from view until it finally disappears. The pattern now fills in where the larger square exists and you see an unbroken background in your peripheral vision.

Observations & Suggestions

What happens when you make the red square in the center larger as in Figure 2? What happens when you make the background smaller as in Figure 3?

This illusion is called a filling-in illusion because your brain replaces the red square with the background pattern. If your brain didn't fill in for your eyes, you would always see a gap where your blind spot is.

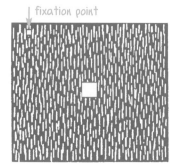

fixation point

Figure 1

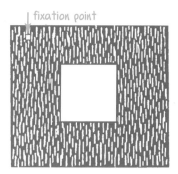

fixation point

Figure 2

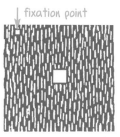

fixation point

Figure 3

Key Words: visual illusions

FADING AWAY ILLUSIONS

CHALLENGE LEVEL

MATERIALS AND EQUIPMENT

- focus circles (see below)
- sheet of white paper

What happens to your vision when you stare? Try gazing steadily at a blob to find out.

Method of Investigation

1. Cover Figure 2 with a sheet of white paper.

2. Close one eye and stare at the dark dot in the center of the circular smudge in Figure 1. What happens after about 10 seconds? What happens when you look away and quickly look back?

Observations & Suggestions

The smudge fades and disappears as the white background fills in. The gradual change from dark to white is too subtle for your eye to be able to maintain the distinction. When you focus on the dot, you are holding your gaze as steady as possible. Your eyeball, however, can never hold perfectly still. It will make tiny tremors. These tiny movements are not enough to keep the image "alive" for your brain. Any larger motion would make the image reappear before it disappeared again.

If you put a circle of dark broken lines around the outer limit of the smudge as in Figure 2, the area is defined and there is enough contrast to prevent the background from completely fading away.

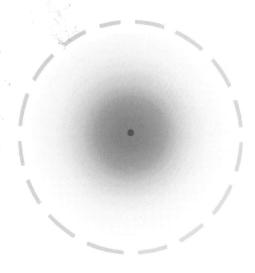

Figure 1

Figure 2

Key Words: fading away illusions · visual illusions

LIGHT

CHALLENGE LEVEL

MATERIALS AND EQUIPMENT

● computer screen

H ow does your eye adjust to light? Do the following experiment to find out.

Method of Investigation

Stand by a light switch while looking at a computer monitor. You need to be at least 6 feet away from the computer. Turn off the lights and stare at the screen, trying not to blink. Keep watching while you switch on the light. Notice that the screen appears to get dimmer.

Observations & Suggestions

The screen does not change in brightness. The difference is in your eyes! The irises in your eyes open and close your pupils to let in different amounts of light. When things are very bright, your pupils become very small. In dim light or in the dark, your pupils expand to let in more light.

In this experiment, you start off in a dim room, so your pupils are enlarged to let in as much light as possible. The light from the screen makes it look quite bright. When you turn on the lights, the increase in light causes your pupils to contract. As a result, less light from the computer screen comes into your eyes and the screen appears to become dimmer than it was.

EYE

IRIS

PUPIL

LENS

RETINA

FOVEA

CONES

OPTIC NERVE

LIGHT

BLIND SPOT

RODS

Key Words: brightness illusions · light adaptation · dark adaptation

CHALLENGE LEVEL

DARK

MATERIALS AND EQUIPMENT

- black construction paper or cloth
- masking tape

How different is your vision in bright light compared to dim light? Look like a pirate to discover the answer. Do this experiment in the evening.

Method of Investigation

Fashion an eye patch out of black construction paper or cloth. Attach it over one eye with masking tape. Wear it for twenty minutes in a well-lit room while you go about your normal activities. Then turn off the lights and remove the eye patch. Look around the room. Notice the difference in vision between your eyes. While you still notice the difference, turn the lights on again. How long does it take before both eyes are equally adapted to the light?

Observations & Suggestions

This experiment shows the difference between an eye that is adapted for bright light and an eye that is adapted to dim light or darkness. We have two kinds of vision—light adapted and dark adapted. This is because there are two kinds of nerve cells at the back of the retina. Only *cones* are located in the center of the back of the eye in an area called the *fovea*. Cones require bright light and are necessary for color vision. *Rods* and fewer cones surround the fovea and are responsible for night vision.

The way your eyes change when they are exposed to bright light and then darkness has been measured extensively by scientists. You experience the first stage when you enter a movie theater after being out in the sunshine. At first, you can't see guiding lights in the aisles unless you look directly at them. This stage lasts about three or four minutes until it levels off. Ten minutes after you first enter the theater, the second stage begins. Then you begin to make out where the seats are. When you are fully dark adapted, a process that takes about twenty-eight minutes, you are seeing as well as you can possibly see in dim light. Your eyes are now thousands of times more sensitive to light than they are in the sunshine. However, your vision is more limited because rods don't distinguish details as well as cones.

When you enter bright light after being fully dark adapted, you experience pain. Your pupils are wide-open and your eyes are extremely sensitive to light. Most of us squint to cut down on the amount of light reaching our eyes. Within twenty seconds, your sensitivity decreases (after a considerable amount of blinking). After three minutes you are fully light adapted.

Key Words: dark adaption · rods and cones

CHALLENGE LEVEL

AMBIGUOUS FIGURES

MATERIALS AND EQUIPMENT

- ambiguous diagrams (see below)
- watch

What happens when you look at something that is ambiguous? After the image on the retina reaches your brain, your brain has to make sense of it. This is called *perception.* Perceptual illusions shed light on how your brain organizes visual information.

Method of Investigation

Can you tell if a diagram of a box or cylinder is thrusting toward you or away from you? Look at the diagrams below to find out.

Spontaneously, the images switch back and forth from one position to another. You have no control over the switching images.

You can time the rate it switches for other people. Have your subject say "now" every time he or she sees the image change. Note how quickly the image changes for several subjects. Do people have different rates for seeing alternating images?

Observations & Suggestions

Some people have suggested that the rate at which an image switches back and forth is a measure of creativity. Can you design an experiment to test this hypothesis?

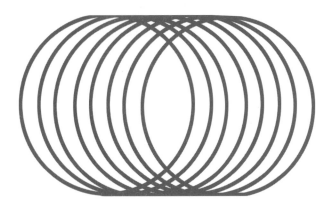

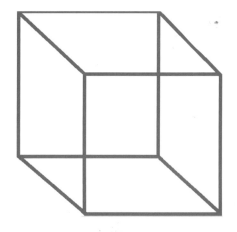

Key Words: ambiguous figure illusions

READING THE BLOBS

CHALLENGE LEVEL

- blobs (see below)
- watch or stopwatch

What happens when you look at an abstract pattern with a hidden meaning? The perceptual interpretation of a visual stimulus is very rapid if you have experience with the stimulus. This is especially true with reading. You can't help reading words when you see them. The Stroop illusion demonstrates this (see page 19). But what if you could slow down the perceptual process? That's what the blobs are designed to do.

Method of Investigation

Examine the blobs. As you look at them, four words will emerge. Don't try to figure them out. Your brain will do the work without any effort on your part. Once you've figured out the blobs, you will never see them as blobs again.

Observations & Suggestions

Show the blobs to other people. See how long it takes for them to see the words. Do all people organize the visual image at the same rate?

Do you think a visually creative person, like an artist, will see the words more quickly than someone who reads all the time? Experiment to find out.

BY PERMISSION OF DAVID LANDRIGON

Key Words: visual perception · perceptual organization

CHALLENGE LEVEL

REACTION TIME

MATERIALS AND EQUIPMENT

- pencil
- tracing or copy machine paper
- scissors
- paste
- oak tag or cardboard
- a friend or two

How fast do your eye and hand react? Maybe you've tried this fun activity. A friend holds a dollar bill vertically. You keep your thumb and forefinger open at the bottom of the bill. Your friend drops the bill and you try to catch it by closing your fingers. The next experiment is a variation on this activity, and you can actually measure reaction time.

Method of Investigation

1 Trace or copy the drawing of the bat with its number scale from page 29. Cut it out and paste it onto stiff cardboard or oaktag and cut it out again.

2 Hold the end of the bat so that it is hanging vertically. Have your friend put his or her forefinger and thumb around, but not touching, the other end of the bat.

3 Instruct your friend to catch the bat when you drop it. The scale on the bat shows the number of seconds it takes for the bat to fall through a certain distance. Where your friend's fingers land on the bat is a measure of his or her reaction time.

Observations & Suggestions

Compare your reaction time with your friends. Do a study of the reaction times of older people. In general, do people seem to lose quickness of reaction time as they get older?

You can't do this test on yourself. Your proprioceptive sense is too much of a giveaway. You don't even need to keep your eyes open to successfully catch a bat you've dropped.

Key Words: reaction time

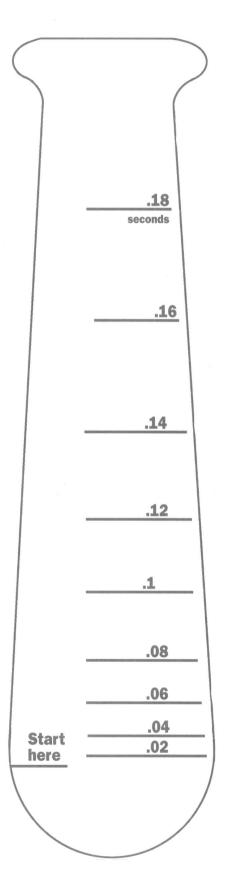

.18
seconds

.16

.14

.12

.1

.08

.06

.04

Start here .02

A 90-mile-an-hour fastball travels to home plate in just .46 seconds. It takes a good batter about .28 seconds to swing and make contact with the ball. This means that in order to hit the ball, the batter must see the ball coming and decide whether or not to swing after just .13 seconds of the ball's flight. Is your reaction time that good?

YOUR FAVORITE SIDE

CHALLENGE LEVEL

MATERIALS AND EQUIPMENT

- lots of friends and family members as subjects
- a copy of the data sheet on page 31 for each person you test
- a pencil and paper for each subject
- scissors and paper
- a fork
- a cup of water
- a ball
- stairs
- a coin
- empty paper towel or toilet tissue tube
- a small box

Most people have a favorite hand that they use for most of the things they do. If you are left-handed, you're in the minority—only one in about every ten people is left-handed. Actually, many people are not totally left-handed or right-handed. They may favor one hand or another depending on the task. There is no standard way to measure handedness. But I've included a simple test, plus a test for your favorite foot, eye, and ear. Give this test to your friends and family to find out what their strong sides are.

Scientists have been studying handedness for about 160 years. Some of the questions they have looked into are: What percent of the population is right-handed? What causes a person to be right-handed or left-handed? Does handedness run in families? Now you can do your own study.

Note: Don't tell your subjects what you are testing.

Method of Investigation

For handedness, note which hand is used for the following activities:

1 Ask your subject to write his or her name.

2 Ask your subject to use scissors to cut a piece of paper.

3 Ask your subject to pick up a fork as if he or she were going to eat.

4 Place a cup of water on the table. Ask your subject to take a sip. Which hand picks up the cup?

5 Which hand is used to throw a ball?

For footedness, note which foot is preferred in the following activities:

1 Ask your subject to kick a ball.

2 Have your subject stand with both feet on the ground in front of a step. Ask him or her to step on to the first stair. (Note: if you don't have any stairs, stretch a piece of string along the ground and ask your subject to step over it.)

3 Put a coin on the floor and ask your subject to step on it.

For eyedness, note which eye is preferred for the following activities:

1 Ask your subject to look through an empty paper towel tube. Which eye is the tube held against?

2 Which eye is used to "sight" an object? Ask your subject to look at a small object on the other side of the room, like a clock on the wall. Now ask your subject to extend an index finger in front of the eyes so that when the finger is looked at the object is blocked. Next ask your subject to open and close each eye. When your subject closes one eye, the object will remain blocked. However, when looked at with the other eye, the finger will appear to "jump" out of the way. The eye that is actually sighting the object is the one that remains blocked. That is the preferred eye.

One scientist claims that you can tell if a person is right-handed or left-handed by examining his or her thumbnails. The hand with the larger and squarer nail is supposedly the dominant hand. Can you design an experiment to check this out?

RIGHT SIDE/LEFT SIDE DATA TABLE

Make a copy of this table for each subject. Place a check mark in the box for the hand, foot, eye, or ear that your subject uses in each test.

Part of Body	Test	Right Side	Left Side
Hand	Write name		
	Use scissors		
	Fork to mouth		
	Drink from cup		
	Throw a ball		
Foot	Kick ball		
	Step up stair		
	Step on coin		
Eye	Look in tube		
	Sight a finger		
	Look through hole		
Ear	Listen to whisper		
	Listen to box		
	Listen at wall		

3 Cut a small circle, the size of a quarter, out of the middle of a piece of paper. Ask your subject to look through the hole with both eyes at a distant object. The paper should then be brought closer and closer to his or her face until only one eye is looking at the object. The eye the hole ends up in front of is the preferred eye.

For earedness, note which ear is preferred for the following activities:

1 Tell your subject that you are going to whisper something very quietly and he or she is to "cup one ear" to enable them to hear better. The ear that's cupped is the preferred ear.

continued on next page ▶

2 Put a small, closed box in front of your subject. Say, "See if you can identify the sound coming from the box by putting it next to your ear." The ear they put the box next to is the preferred ear.

3 Ask your subject to put an ear to a wall to listen to the next room. The ear that's placed next to the wall is the preferred ear.

Observations & Suggestions

Collect and analyze your results. The more people you test, the more accurate your results. How many people in your test are right-handed and how many are left-handed?

A person can be considered right-handed if there were more right-sided responses than left-sided. The same is true for footedness, eyedness, and earedness. Calculate percentages by dividing the number of subjects who exhibited a particular sidedness into the total number of subjects and multiply by 100.

Here are the results from a scientist who did this experiment:

	Strongly left-sided	Strongly right-sided	Mixed-sided
Handedness	5%	72%	22%
Footedness	4%	46%	50%
Eyedness	5%	54%	41%
Earedness	15%	35%	60%

How do your results compare?

Another study says that 11% of all Americans are left-handed, but the results are not that simple. Here is a breakdown: Men are more likely (12.6%) to be left-handed than women (9.9%). Young people (10–20 years old) are more likely to be left-handed (14% for males, 12% for females) than are older people (near 6% for both sexes).

Does left-handedness run in families? When you find a left-handed person, ask if you can do a family tree for left-handedness. Statistics say that if both parents are right-handed, the chances of a child being left-handed are 9.5%. If one parent is left-handed, there is a 19.5% chance of their child being left-handed. If both parents are left-handed, they have a 26.1% chance of having a left-handed child.

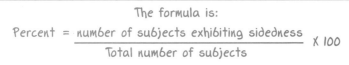

The formula is:
$$Percent = \frac{number\ of\ subjects\ exhibiting\ sidedness}{Total\ number\ of\ subjects} \times 100$$

Key Words: sidedness · handedness

HAIR

Examining the Cuticle (pg. 33) · Testing the Cortex (pg. 34)

Under a microscope, a hair cuticle (the outside of a hair) looks something like fish scales with irregular edges. In healthy hair (hair that has not been treated with chemicals), the scales overlap and lie flat against each other. Only the ends of the scales are visible. The cuticle averages between seven and ten scales thick. The ends of the scales point away from the root of the hair. You can feel this. Hold a single hair from your head so that it is taut. Run the thumb and index finger of your other hand back and forth along this hair. Notice that there is no resistance to this motion when moving from the root toward the end. But there is some friction when you move in the opposite direction. That's because your fingers are rubbing against the ends of the cuticle scales. The sound you hear when your rub hairs together is due to the rough cuticle scales rubbing against each other.

CHALLENGE LEVEL

EXAMINING THE CUTICLE

MATERIALS AND EQUIPMENT

- several untreated hairs (You can ask a local hairdresser to collect hair samples for you.)
- several chemically treated hairs (bleached or permanented or both)
- 2 shallow bowls of water

The job of the cuticle is to protect the hair cortex. Its rough surface traps and holds sebum, an oily material produced by glands to make hair waterproof. The direction of the scales helps water run off the ends of the hair and protects the cortex from absorbing too much moisture. What happens to the cuticle when hair is bleached or permed? Experiment to find out.

Method of Investigation

Put a few untreated hairs in one bowl of water and a few chemically treated hairs in the other. Watch to see which sinks first.

Observations & Suggestions

The untreated hairs will float. The protective coating on the hair and the tightly packed cuticle scales keep the water from wetting the hair. The hair floats due to surface tension of water in much the same way as a needle can "float" on the surface of water. But the treated hair will quickly sink, because water is able to wet it more quickly.

Key Words: hair cuticle · damaged hair · sebum · hair and structure

TESTING THE CORTEX

MATERIALS AND EQUIPMENT

- transparent tape
- several hairs about 5 inches long
- paper clip
- several keys
- postage balance (optional)
- ruler

How strong is a hair? How elastic is it? These properties depend on the cortex, or entral shaft, of a hair. The cortex is 75% to 90% of the weight of a hair. It is made of many millions of parallel fibers of hard keratin, a tough, insoluble protein, that are twisted around each other as in a rope. The following experiment demonstrates that the cortex is the source of hair's basic properties.

Method of Investigation

A healthy, undamaged hair is strong. It should be able to support up to 2 ounces of weight without breaking. Here's how you can test the strength of a hair:

1 Tape one end of a hair to a smooth surface.

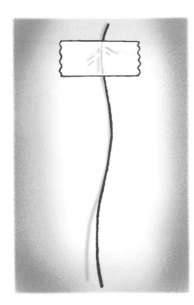

2 Stick a paper clip through a key.

3 Pass the free end of the hanging hair through the paper clip to form a loop.

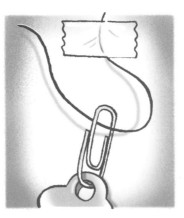

4 Tape the ends together as shown in the picture. Let the hair hang with the key. Does it break?

5 If it doesn't break, hang a second key on the paper clip. Keep adding keys, one by one, until the hair snaps. Take off the last key you added before the hair snapped. Weigh the keys and paper clip. This weight is slightly less than the weight the hair can support without snapping.

Hair stretches more easily when it is wet. The humidity of the shower should cause the hair to stretch several millimeters. The response of hair to moisture has been used to measure humidity in the air. The instrument that does this is called a "hair hygrometer." Some weather stations use hair hygrometers to measure changes in humidity.

6 The length of hair changes when it is wet. Tape a new hair to a towel rack in the bathroom and hang a single key on the end. Measure the exact length of the loop. (Since millimeters are very small units of measurement, you will be most accurate if you measure your hair loop in millimeters.) Turn on the shower and let the bathroom steam up. Measure the hair again in the steamy bathroom.

Observations & Suggestions

The hairs I tested supported about 1½ ounces before snapping. You can test hairs from different people. Ask your long-haired friends for samples. Red hair is coarser than black, brown, or blond. Is it stronger? Some people will obviously have stronger hair than others, but you can see why human hair has been twisted together to make ropes for heavy lifting.

You can use these procedures to compare the differences in hair strength and elasticity. How does bleached hair compare to unbleached? Curly and straight hair? Blond vs. red vs. brown?

Key Words: hair cortex · human hair · hair and tensile strength

CHAPTER 2

Inspirations from the Supermarket

Your supermarket can be the source of more than one kind of inspiration. In addition to whetting your appetite for food, it can provide almost unlimited ideas and materials for science projects. It can also provide equipment to do experiments. Just stroll up and down the aisles—look at packaging, look at food contents, and let your imagination ask questions.

Buy vegetables for the colors you'll extract from them, buy blue cheese to grow penicillin, ask the deli manager for small plastic containers, get a few extra Styrofoam® trays from the meat department. Pick up an assortment of seeds to sprout, including parrot food, dried beans, and birdseed. If the contents of your shopping basket look odd, let people wonder what kind of meal you're preparing. You can tell them it's food for thought!

A MEAL FOR MOLD

MATERIALS AND EQUIPMENT

- 3 small plastic containers and lids from the supermarket deli department (about 4½ inches in diameter)
- knife
- 3 pieces of white bread
- measuring spoons
- water
- labels
- pen or pencil
- sugar
- 2 measuring cups
- fresh blue cheese

It takes more than a discovery by one scientist to make a miracle drug available. After Alexander Fleming discovered penicillin in bread mold, people suffered and died from infections for another ten years. A big stumbling block was finding a way to grow great quantities of the mold. A U.S. Government agricultural laboratory attacked the problem. Dr. Andrew Moyer figured that the answer lay in what the mold liked to "eat." Do your own study of bread mold to see if it likes extra sugar in its diet.

Method of Investigation

1. Make certain that the plastic containers are very clean. If they were used, wash them with a disinfecting dishwasher detergent, rinse well, and air dry. If they've never been used they should still be washed because of their exposure to the air.

2. Cut the crust off each slice of bread so that it fits into the bottom of a plastic container. Use a different container for each piece of bread. Sprinkle one piece of bread with 1 tablespoon of water. Label this container CONTROL.

3. Dissolve 1 tablespoon of sugar in 1 cup of water.

Drop 1 tablespoon of this solution over a second slice of bread. Label this container FULL STRENGTH. Pour ½ cup of the sugar-water solution into a second measuring cup. Add water to make it a full cup. Put 1 tablespoon of this solution on the third slice of bread. Label this container HALF STRENGTH.

4. Now you are going to inoculate your dishes with *Penicillium.* The blue streaks in blue cheese are this mold. Cut out some of the blue mold. You need three pieces of mold that are each the same size as this square: ■!

Put a piece of mold in the center of each slice of bread. Put the covers on the containers, and put them in a dark place. Check the containers every day for a week.

Observations & Suggestions

When I did this experiment, by the fourth day there was a big difference in mold growth between the control and the molds that had sugar. There was also some additional growth of foreign molds. Black bread mold is called *aspergillis niger*. If you have a magnifying glass, look closely at the mold. You may see many tiny threads growing out of the mold.

When Dr. Moyer did his experimenting, he found the mold grew best when he added a by-product of a wet corn-milling process. You might try adding some of the liquid from canned sweet corn, some diluted corn syrup ($\frac{1}{2}$ water, $\frac{1}{2}$ syrup), or some diluted baby formula ($\frac{1}{2}$ water, $\frac{1}{2}$ formula), which contains the milk sugar called *lactose*.

Penicillin, the first antibiotic, was discovered by accident. Alexander Fleming (1881–1955), a Scottish scientist, was studying harmful bacteria in the hope of finding a way to stop them from infecting people. He left an uncovered dish of cultured bacteria lying about his lab for a few days. He was just about to throw it out when he noticed that some specks of mold had also started growing in the dish. What struck Fleming was that around each speck of mold was a clear area where bacteria had died and no new bacteria were growing.

This observation in 1928 led Fleming into intense research: What was the mold? What was the substance produced by the mold? Would it kill other types of harmful bacteria? Would it kill human white blood cells? He discovered that the mold was a form of garden-variety green bread mold known as *Penicillium*. It secreted a chemical that discouraged the growth of many germs but not all. It did not harm human blood cells. But he never isolated the actual substance and never used it to treat infection. That job was accomplished by Dr. Moyer's Lab in Peoria, Illinois, in 1944.

Key Words: penicillium · bread mold

CHALLENGE LEVEL

SEARCHING FOR YEAST BUSTERS

MATERIALS AND EQUIPMENT

- 3 half-liter bottles of bottled water
- funnel
- measuring spoons
- sugar
- labels
- pen or pencil
- baby shampoo
- shampoo containing *ketoconazole* as its active ingredient (Read the labels to find out what's in it.)
- 2 packages of baker's yeast
- 3 identical helium-quality rubber balloons
- string and ruler (optional)

Yeast are one-celled microorganisms related to fungi. The yeast you'll find dried and packaged in the supermarket (called *Saccharomyces cerevisiae*) is used for making bread. Give it some water and a little sugar and it springs into action—using the sugar as food, it begins multiplying itself. In the process, called *fermentation*, the yeast gives off two valuable waste products: alcohol and carbon dioxide. The alcohol is essential to the production of beer and wine. The carbon dioxide is used to make bread and cake rise. (The alcohol evaporates during baking.)

Human skin is host to a type of yeast (called *Pityrosporum ovale*) that normally doesn't bother us. However, an overgrowth of this particular yeast causes the skin on the scalp to react, producing dandruff. One treatment is often found in dandruff shampoos, particularly those that contain the antifungal agent *ketoconazole*. By inhibiting the growth of the yeast, the dandruff is reduced.

Does antidandruff shampoo inhibit fermentation of baker's yeast? Do the next experiment to find out.

Method of Investigation

1. To prepare the *substrate* (the material on which the yeast acts) bottles, empty out about half of the water in each bottle, leaving behind the same amount in each one. (Save the bottle caps.) Using the funnel, add 1 tablespoon of sugar to each bottle. Put the caps on and shake so that the sugar dissolves. Label one bottle CONTROL. Put 2 teaspoons of baby shampoo into the second sugar-water bottle and label this one BABY SHAMPOO. Put 2 teaspoons of antidandruff shampoo into the third bottle and label it ANTIDANDRUFF SHAMPOO.

2. Add 1 teaspoon of dried baker's yeast to each bottle. Put the caps back on the bottles and invert them slowly back and forth to thoroughly mix the contents. Remove the bottle caps and quickly stretch the mouth of a balloon over each bottle top. Make sure that the neck of each balloon

completely covers the screw channels at the top of the bottle. Note the time.

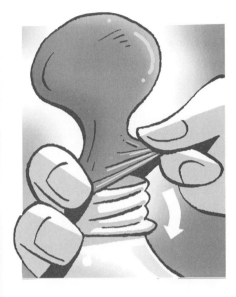

③ Watch your experiment over the next two or three hours. Note the time when each balloon pops into an upright position. After that, you can measure the carbon dioxide production by wrapping a string around the largest part of each balloon. The length of the string gives the circumference of the balloon and therefore a rough measure of how much gas has been produced.

Observations & Suggestions

Which balloon popped up first? Do your results indicate that antidandruff shampoo inhibits yeast action? There are other substances you might try. There are some antifungal preparations for feet and there are antiseptics for cleaning bathrooms. You can also use this technique to try to find the ideal conditions for growing yeast. Change the amount of sugar in each bottle, change the temperature surrounding the bottle (put in a hot-water bath and in ice water). Compare the action of yeast in drinks containing sugar and in drinks with sugar substitutes. Compare sugar with molasses and syrup.

Smell the balloons. Can you smell any alcohol? You wouldn't be able to smell anything if molecules couldn't pass through the balloon. Do you smell anything through the bottle?

Yeast is a one-celled living organism. Baker's yeast uses sugar as food and gives off carbon dioxide and alcohol as waste products. In baking, the carbon dioxide is a leavening agent, that is, it makes breads and cakes rise as the gas makes bubbles in the dough. If you smell the bottles containing yeast, you should smell the alcohol. The process by which yeast creates carbon dioxide and alcohol from sugar is called *fermentation*.

Key Words: yeast · fermentation · ketoconazole

PROTEIN EATERS

MATERIALS AND EQUIPMENT

- an adult helper
- 1 package unflavored gelatin (Knox®, for example)
- a small plastic container from the supermarket deli department (about $4\frac{1}{4}$ inches in diameter)
- measuring cup
- water
- refrigerator
- small plate
- knife
- labels
- pen or pencil
- snack size zip plastic bags
- measuring spoons

Any or all of the following:
- meat tenderizer
- tablet contact lens cleaner
- liquid detergent with enzymes (like Tide®)
- laundry spot remover with enzymes
- fresh pineapple, papaya, figs
- garlic press
- small dishes
- strainer
- large cups

Your body breaks down proteins when you digest them. What protein digesters can you find in the supermarket?

Life would not be possible without a group of chemicals found in living things that control every step of every chemical reaction that contributes to life. These chemical regulators are called *enzymes* because they were first discovered in yeast cells—the word *enzyme* means "in yeast." Enzymes are also proteins, a class of compounds made of chains of small molecules called amino acids. There are about twenty-four amino acids that form the "alphabet" of proteins, which are like paragraphs—each with its own meaning. All organisms must continually make their own proteins, and the source of raw materials is food—other once-living things. Of course, the protein in a food is different from the protein of the food user. So food must be digested—broken down into amino acids—in order to be rebuilt up again into the specific proteins that the food user needs. Since protein digestion is a chemical reaction, there are, as you might have guessed, a group of enzymes that break down protein. These enzymes can be found in a number of products, both natural and manufactured, from your supermarket. In this experiment, you can watch proteins being broken down. Note: This is a fairly involved procedure that can take several days.

Method of Investigation

NOTE: Since you are using the stove, have an adult helper.

1. Prepare the gelatin *substrate*, which is the material on which the enzyme acts. Gelatin is pure protein. Put the unflavored gelatin in the plastic container. Add $\frac{1}{2}$ cup cold water. Let the mixture soften for about ten minutes. Then add 1 cup boiling water. Put in the refrigerator to cool and gel for twenty-four hours.

2. Unmold the gelatin substrate. To do this, set the plastic container in hot water for two or three

minutes. Put a small plate upside down over the top of the plastic container. Invert the plate and container and shake the container so that the gelatin falls out onto the plate.

3 Cut the gelatin into 1-inch cubes. Write a label for each sample you are testing plus the labels DRY CONTROL and WET CONTROL.

4 Put each label along the top of a zip plastic snack-sized bag. Put a cube of gelatin in each bag. After you put in each solution containing the enzyme, zip each bag closed.

5 The DRY CONTROL bag just gets closed with only gelatin and no liquid. Put 1 tablespoon of water in the WET CONTROL bag along with the gelatin cube.

6 Mix ¼ teaspoon meat tenderizer in a small dish with 1 tablespoon water. Pour it into the bag marked MEAT TENDERIZER.

7 Put a tablet of contact lens cleaner into another small dish with 1 table-spoon of water. When it

has dissolved, pour it over the gelatin cube in the bag labeled CONTACT LENS CLEANER.

8 Put 1 tablespoon of liquid Tide® over cube in the bag labeled TIDE.

9 Put 1 tablespoon of laundry spot remover in the appropriately labeled bag.

10 Peel and cut up some of the fresh fruit into small pieces. Compress them through the garlic press into small dishes. You need about 1 tablespoon of juice from each fruit. Strain it as you pour it over the gelatin in the appropriately labeled bag.

11 Tilt all the bags so that both the gelatin cube and the liquid are in the same corner. Set each bag in a large cup. Look at the bags after an hour, then look at them periodically for the next day or so. Look at the size of the gelatin cube, and look at the solution.

Observations & Suggestions

I found that the meat tenderizer had a quick and dramatic effect on the gelatin cube. It disappeared after a few hours. The lens cleaner also had a similar effect. The meat tenderizer made the substrate fall apart, and the lens cleaner had extra material floating in it, making it look cloudy. The Tide made the gelatin square shrink. I think that's because it drew water out of the gelatin. Fresh pineapple, papaya, and fig juice all contain enzymes that digest protein, so in those bags, the cubes disappeared. I also tried sections of hard-boiled egg white and cubes of tofu (a protein from soybeans) in place of the gelatin cubes with similar results.

Do you think temperature can affect enzyme activity? What about how acidic or basic a solution is? Try the experiment again with substrate and meat tenderizer solution, but add a little vinegar to one sample and a little baking soda to the other.

Key Words: enzyme · amino acids · meat tenderizer · papain · bromelian

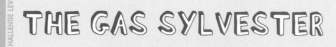

THE GAS SYLVESTER

MATERIALS AND EQUIPMENT

Carbon dioxide gas shows up in lots of food and drink. What are its properties? Get to know it more personally in the next series of experiments.

Carbon dioxide was once known as "the gas sylvester." "Sylvester" comes from a Latin word meaning "woods" or "forest" because the gas was found in caves containing rotting wood. The gas formed a layer on the floor of the caves, and since there was no wind to blow it away it stayed close to the ground. There are stories of dogs that died when they went into such caves. They suffocated to death because this mysterious gas displaced the air. The strange thing was that a person accompanying the dog was not harmed. No one realized that a human's head was above the surface of the gas.

- plastic clay (like Plasticine®)
- 12-inch length of plastic tubing from an aquarium store
- unopened bottle of soda pop
- large wash basin ⅔ full of water
- several small jars (jelly jars, for example)
- small bowl of hot tap water
- a plastic cover for each small jar (such as plastic covers from coffee cans or tennis ball cans)
- measuring cup
- 2 empty half-liter soda pop bottles
- measuring spoons
- sugar
- yeast
- baking soda
- vinegar
- kitchen matches
- candle
- birthday cake candles
- pipe cleaners or wire

Method of Investigation

Collecting Carbon Dioxide from Soda:

1. First set up your apparatus to collect carbon dioxide from a fresh bottle of soda. Pinch off a wad of clay and stick one end of the plastic tubing through it so that ½ inch comes out the other end.

2. Open the bottle of soda and mold the wad of clay into an airtight stopper by pushing it into the mouth of the bottle. The short end of the tube should be above the

liquid in the bottle. Put the other end of the tubing in the large basin of water. Do you see bubbles coming out of the end of the tubing? Don't worry if you don't see them yet.

③ Submerge one of the small jars in the basin, completely filling it with water. Turn the jar upside down and rest it on the bottom of the basin until you're ready. There should be no air pockets in the jar.

④ Now drive off the gas in the soda. To do this, stand the soda bottle in the small bowl of hot tap water. Watch the end of your delivery tube in the basin. By now, bubbles should be coming from the tube. Let the bubbles rise for a few minutes to drive out the air in the bottle and the tube.

⑤ To collect the gas, hold the inverted, water-filled collecting jar in the basin over the delivery tube as shown in the picture. The bubbles will rise to the surface and drive out the water from the jar back into the basin. This method of collecting a gas is called *displacement of water*. When you have completely filled the jar with gas, bubbles will form in the water outside the jar and rise to the surface.

Carbon dioxide in soda is in a solution. A gas will dissolve in liquid, especially if it's under pressure. The pressure is released when you open a bottle or a can of soda. Bubbles of gas come out of the solution and rush to the surface. Gas is less soluble in a liquid as the temperature increases. That's why the gas is driven off by putting the soda bottle in hot water.

⑥ Still holding the gas-filled jar upside down

continued on next page ▶

The chemical name for baking soda is *sodium bicarbonate* and the chemical name for vinegar is *acetic acid*. When you mix the two, they react to form water, carbon dioxide, and sodium acetate. The chemical release of carbon dioxide is also used by bakers. Recipes that call for baking soda usually have some acid in the recipe such as sour milk (with lactic acid), cream of tartar (with tartaric acid) or lemon juice (citric acid).

and under water, remove the delivery tube from the jar, leaving the tube in the basin, and slide a plastic disk across the mouth of the jar. (Be careful not to tilt the jar, or water will rush in, driving out your precious gas.) Hold the disk in place as you remove the inverted jar from the water. Turn the jar right side up when you have removed it from the basin. Set aside with the lid on. Collect more jars of gas until there is no more fizz coming from the soda.

Collecting Carbon Dioxide from Yeast:

1 Generate carbon dioxide from yeast fermentation. Put 1 cup of water in a clean, empty soda bottle. Add 1 tablespoon of sugar and 1 teaspoon of dried yeast. Put the bottle cap on and shake well to mix. Remove the bottle cap and push your clay plug stopper with tubing in the top as before.

2 Place the bottle in a bowl of warm tap water. Put the tubing in the basin. Watch the bubbles coming off. Let it bubble for about ten minutes before you start collecting the gas. Collect a jar or two of gas from the yeast.

Collecting Carbon Dioxide from a Chemical Reaction:

Put 1 tablespoon of baking soda in a clean, empty soda bottle. Add ½ cup of vinegar. Quickly insert the plug with the tube. This reaction will happen quickly. Add more baking soda when it stops. Collect a jar or two of gas.

Observations & Suggestions

NOTE: Since you are using matches, this experiment requires an adult helper.

Now you're ready to test the carbon dioxide you've collected. Strike a match and lower it into one of the jars you collected from the soda. After you see what happens, cover the jar again. Then repeat this test with a jar collected from the yeast and with one from the vinegar and baking soda reaction. What happens in each case?

Light a candle and make a pouring motion over it with a jar of gas you just used to put out the match. Again the fire is doused.

You have just discovered two important things about the gas in the jar: It puts out a flame and it is heavier than air. (That's the reason you can pour it.) If it were lighter than air, it would escape up into the air if left to stand in an open jar. Check this out. Take the lid off a jar and let it stand for a few minutes without a cover. Repeat the tests with the match and the candle with this jar. Usually this heavier-than-air gas will stay put for about half an hour before spilling up into the air. If your room is drafty, however, the gas may empty more quickly.

Do you notice any difference between the gas samples you collected from the different sources?

Here's still another fun thing to do. Make a wire candleholder for a birthday candle with a pipe cleaner or some picture-hanging wire, as shown in the picture. Make sure the candle is held securely in a vertical position. Lower the lit candle slowly into one of the jars of gas. If you keep the candle perfectly vertical, the flame stays at the mouth of the jar, separated from the wick beneath it. A thin column of smoke trails from the wick to the invisible surface of the gas where the burning takes place. You've separated the flame from its wick! The gas in the jar extinguishes the flame, but a stream of hot wax rises from the wick. When it reaches the surface of the gas in the jar (which you can't see, of course) the hot wax burns because it is in the air.

Key Words: carbon dioxide and properties · sodium bicarbonate

CHALLENGE LEVEL

A SPROUTING OUTING

MATERIALS AND EQUIPMENT

Alfalfa and Chinese bean sprouts are not the only baby plants you can find at the supermarket. You just have to know how to look for them. I get a kick out of prowling up and down the supermarket aisles looking for products I can use in a way most people never think of. I found more than thirty different kinds of seeds to sprout. How many can you find?

Method of Investigation

1. If one of your sources of seeds is a mixture, such as parrot food, read the label to see what kinds of seeds are in it. Sort the seeds into groups. Save and label a seed from each group as a reference. See if you can identify what seeds you have.

2. Fold a paper towel in quarters so that it fits in the bottom of a plastic deli container. Moisten it thoroughly with water. It should be soaked through but not dripping wet. Place it in the container.

3. Put several seeds on it. Cover the seeds with another folded and moistened paper towel. Put the lid on it and label the lid with the source of the seeds and the type of seed, if possible.

- seeds from the supermarket (here's a list to get you started):
    - popcorn
    - birdseed
    - dill seed
    - caraway seed
    - dried peas
    - dried beans
    - poppy seed
    - parrot food
    - whole (not roasted) peanuts
- paper towels
- small plastic containers and lids from the supermarket deli department (about $4\frac{1}{4}$ inches in diameter)
- plenty of water
- labels
- pen

4 Check your seeds every day. Some seeds will start sprouting sooner than others.

Observations & Suggestions

Which seeds started sprouting first, the small ones or the large ones? By day five, mine were going strong. Look carefully at a sprouting seed. The first thing that starts growing is the seed root. As it gets longer, tiny rootlets sprout off the main root. They show up as white fuzz. Look more closely at them with a magnifying glass. The seed leaf, called a *cotyledon*, appears next. Some plants have only one seed leaf and are called *monocotyledons* (monocots, for short). Most birdseed, wheat, corn, and grasses are all monocots. Other plants—like beans, peas, and peanuts—have two seed leaves and are called *dicotyledons* (dicots, for short).

In which direction do the seed roots grow and in which direction do the seed leaves grow? It's awesome how plants know the difference between up and down. On day five, I turned the dish growing the birdseed upside down. The results by the next day were amazing.

Did any of your spice seeds sprout? (Mine didn't.) It makes you wonder if spice producers somehow kill the seeds when they process them.

You can also try sprouting seeds and pits from fruit. To get an avocado seed going, stick three or four toothpicks into it about ¾ inch above the flatter end. Rest the toothpicks on the rim of a glass and fill it with water so that the bottom of the pit is covered. Keep the glass out of bright sunlight and replace any evaporated water over the next several days so that

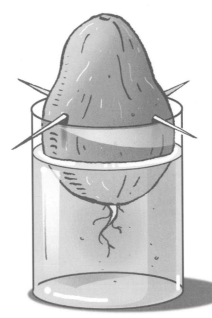

the pit bottom is always in water. Some pits will take as long as one and a half months to sprout, so be patient. Let the roots and main stem grow until the stem is about 8 inches tall. Then cut the stem off about 3 inches from the seed so that the roots get stronger. Plant your avocado in a pot with soil two weeks after you cut it back.

Try sprouting apple and pear seeds the same way you did the dried seeds. They may take up to a month or more. Be sure to keep the paper towels moist. Watch for mold and throw away moldy seeds.

Beet and carrot tops can sprout like avocado seeds. Place the cut tops in a shallow dish of water. Roots will develop and leaves will come out of the top. Stick three toothpicks in the sides of a piece of fresh ginger root. Rest the toothpicks on the rim of a small glass custard cup. Add water to cover the bottom of the root. Wait. It may take months, but you will see a bud coming out of the other end of the root. Replace the water every few days.

Key Words: cotyledon · sprouting seeds · avocado seed

THE COLORS OF FRUITS AND VEGETABLES

Part 1: Extract the Pigments (pg. 50) · Part 2: Analyze the Pigments (pg. 51) · Vegetable Dyes (pg. 53)

What chemicals make plants green, yellow, red, purple, orange, and every shade in between? The first problem is to extract the pigments, the next is to analyze them. The methods here answer such questions as: Is the green in all plants due to the same pigment? What do red and blue pigments have in common? Are there any hidden pigments in some plants that are masked by the obvious color?

CHALLENGE LEVEL

PART 1: EXTRACT THE PIGMENTS

MATERIALS AND EQUIPMENT

- an assortment of fruits and vegetables: spinach, parsley, kale, orange pepper, oranges, yams, carrots, red pepper, red onion, red cabbage, beets, blueberries, or red grapes
- garlic press
- measuring spoons
- small containers (like glass custard cups or plastic salad dressing cups from the supermarket deli department)
- colorless nail polish remover or rubbing alcohol
- water
- blender or food processor (optional)

Method of Investigation

1. To get the green pigments out of a spinach leaf, squish the leaf through a garlic press. Do this several times until you have about 2 tablespoons of chopped-up leaf. Put the crushed leaves into a small dish and cover it with nail polish remover. Let it sit for a few hours, mushing it around every once in a while.

2. Yellow and orange pigments should also be extracted by crushing the vegetables or fruits through a garlic press and covering the mashed material with nail polish remover or rubbing alcohol.

3. Red pigments dissolve in water. Crush red cabbage

leaves, blueberries, and other red and blue fruits and vegetables into a small dish. Add a little water or a small amount of rubbing alcohol.

Now, on to Part 2.

Key Words: plant pigments · chromatography

PART 2: ANALYZE THE PIGMENTS

CHALLENGE LEVEL

MATERIALS AND EQUIPMENT

- an adult helper
- iron
- wraparound coffee filters —these are not cone or basket coffee filters
- scissors
- pencils
- transparent tape
- clear, 10-ounce drinking glasses
- plant pigment extracts from previous experiment
- wooden toothpicks
- hair dryer
- water or rubbing alcohol

Scientists use a method called *chromatography*, which means "to write with color," as a way of seeing what plant pigments are present. Once you have extracted your plant pigments, you are now ready to analyze them. Do colored plant extracts contain more than one pigment? You can separate them to find out. Here's how to do it:

Method of Investigation

NOTE: Since you are using an iron, have an adult helper.

1. Prepare strips of filter paper to run your tests on. Iron a square of wraparound coffee filter paper so that there are no creases in it. Cut a strip about 1 inch wide. Make sure that there are no holes in the strip (the filter paper already has tiny holes in it). Wrap one end of the strip around a pencil and tape it in place. Cut the strip so that the bottom is ¼ inch above the bottom of a 10-ounce glass when the pencil rests on the top of the glass. (See illustration.)

2. Draw a horizontal pencil line across the strip about 1 inch from the bottom. This line will be the starting point for the pigment.

3. Apply a drop of plant pigment to the line by dipping a toothpick into some plant extract and touching it to the filter paper. Dry the spot with a hair dryer. Repeat, applying more plant extract to the same spot, drying it in between applications, until you have a nice dark spot of plant pigment about ¼ inch in diameter. This takes patience!

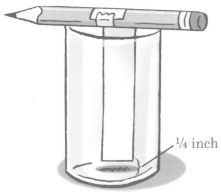

¼ inch

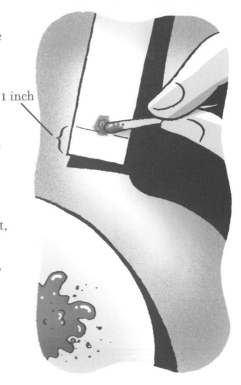

1 inch

continued on next page ▶

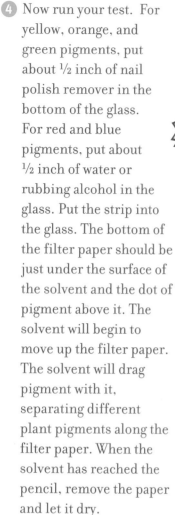

4 Now run your test. For yellow, orange, and green pigments, put about ½ inch of nail polish remover in the bottom of the glass. For red and blue pigments, put about ½ inch of water or rubbing alcohol in the glass. Put the strip into the glass. The bottom of the filter paper should be just under the surface of the solvent and the dot of pigment above it. The solvent will begin to move up the filter paper. The solvent will drag pigment with it, separating different plant pigments along the filter paper. When the solvent has reached the pencil, remove the paper and let it dry.

Green plant pigments are called *chlorophyll*. They enable plants to manufacture sugar from carbon dioxide and water in the presence of light. This process is known as *photosynthesis*. There are two main chlorophylls—one is bright green and one is olive green.

Yellow, orange and red pigments are called *carotenoids* because they were first isolated from carrots. There are always several different carotenoids found together with other pigments including chlorophyll. A yellow carotenoid will separate first from chlorophyll.

Red and blue pigments are called *anthocyanins*. The actual color in a plant depends on how much acid or base there is in the plant cells. Red cabbage juice changes color in an acid and a base. Add a little baking soda to turn it blue, add vinegar to turn it pink. Anthocyanins dissolve in water and alcohol.

Observations & Suggestions

You can use chromatography to identify a pigment in two ways: by its color and by the distance it travels. A solvent will drag along lightweight pigments faster than heavier ones. In analyzing green plant pigment, you'll find that the carotenoid separated out from the chlorophylls first and must be a much lighter molecule than the green pigments lagging behind it.

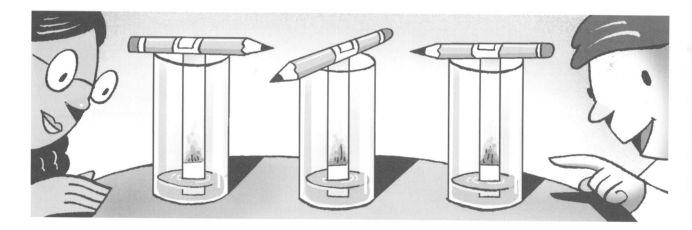

Key Words: chromatography · chlorophyll · anthocyanins · carotenoids

CHALLENGE LEVEL

VEGETABLE DYES

MATERIALS
AND
EQUIPMENT

Can you extract the pigments that color vegetables and use them to color fabric?

Method of Investigation

NOTE: Since you will be using a grater, have an adult helper present.

1. Spread newspapers on the table, wear old clothes that can get stained or an apron.

2. To get the pigment out of the plant, grate about ¼ cup of vegetable onto a plate. This breaks up the cells, releasing the pigment. (Caution: A grater can scrape your fingers if you're not careful.)

3. Place the pigment in a plastic bag and add about ¼ cup of warm water. Zip the bag closed and gently massage it for about three minutes so that the water becomes well colored.

4. Open a corner of the bag and pour out just the water into a plastic cup.

5. Repeat steps 2, 3, and 4 with each vegetable.

6. Cut a strip of each kind of cloth and a strip of paper about 1 inch wide and 6 inches long. Make a strip of each material for every color you're testing.

7. Submerge a strip of each material into the dye and let them soak overnight. Remove them the next day and spread them out on paper towels to dry.

8. See how well the dye molecules stay in the fabric when it is washed. Fill clean plastic cups halfway with warm water. Put the strips in the cups and move them up and down. Which sample loses the most color? Add some detergent. Which dyes remained even after soap was added?

Observations & Suggestions

Natural dyes must bond with the molecules of fabric fibers. They do not bond as well with synthetic fabrics. Synthetic dyes have been developed for modern fabrics. In ancient times, when only natural dyes were used, people also used only natural fibers from cotton, flax (linen), and wool. Not only did these colors run when washed, but they also faded in sunlight. Put some naturally dyed strips in sunlight and see what happens to the colors over time.

- an adult helper
- newspapers
- old clothes or an apron
- grater
- raw vegetables with strong color: carrots, beets, red cabbage, sweet potatoes
- small plates
- measuring cup
- zip plastic bags
- warm water
- plastic cups
- scissors
- white 100% cotton cloth (from a clean old rag, check the label if possible)
- white cotton/synthetic blend cloth (from a clean old rag, check the label if possible)
- white paper
- paper towels
- laundry detergent

MAKE YOUR OWN COLD CEREAL

Crisp Little Rice (pg. 54) · Flakes (pg. 56)

Cereal grains—oats, wheat, corn, rice—have been food since long before recorded history. They are all seeds and can be stored without spoiling to be eaten at some later time. This was especially important when there was no refrigeration. The problem with seeds, of course, is that they're tough on the teeth. This was a challenge to human ingenuity. Seeds are boiled (to make porridge), ground into flour, crushed, or heated and popped. The only seeds that really pop well are popcorn and amaranth. (Amaranth can be found in health food stores.) Popcorn was the first cold breakfast cereal, served, in colonial America, floating in milk. Today there is an endless variety of cold cereals sold as flakes, puffs, squares, o's, loops, balls, and tiny crisp shapes.

CHALLENGE LEVEL

CRISP LITTLE RICE

MATERIALS AND EQUIPMENT

- an adult helper
- ½ cup dry rice
- water
- pot
- colander
- cookie sheet
- oven
- measuring spoons
- vegetable oil
- frying pan
- spatula
- paper towels

Rice is very dry. Can you make it pop if you put water into the seeds?

Method of Investigation

NOTE: Since you will be using the stove and frying with hot oil, have an adult present for this experiment.

1 Put water into the rice by cooking it according to the directions on the package.

The commercial cereal, Rice Krispies®, is made from milled white rice, not unlike white rice you cook for dinner. It is first cooked, then dried to have a controlled moisture content. After being slightly flattened by passing between two rollers, it is toasted. This makes the rice kernels swell up and turn brown.

2 Drain the cooked rice and spread it on a cookie sheet so that it is one layer thick. Bake in a 200°F oven for at least one hour or until the rice appears to be dry. Stir several times during the drying process. You are now drying the rice from the outside in.

3 Put a few tablespoons of vegetable oil in a frying pan. Heat the oil for a few minutes. Carefully add rice to the frying pan. If the oil is too hot, it may spatter. Within a few seconds, the rice will sound like it's popping and start to swell.

Use the spatula to remove the popped rice to a paper towel to drain off the oil. Eat with milk and sugar or just as it is.

Observations & Suggestions

When you cook the rice, water swells each kernel. When you fry the dried rice, the small amount of water left in the rice turns to steam, expands, and causes the starch around it to swell into a chamber. Instead of the whole seed popping like corn, only small areas along the grain of rice pop. You might try to see if you can get it to puff in a toaster oven.

Key Words: rice cereal · rice and history

FLAKES

CHALLENGE LEVEL

MATERIALS AND EQUIPMENT

- an adult helper
- small bowls
- measuring spoons
- whole-wheat flour
- water
- aluminum foil
- toaster overn
- cornmeal
- cornstarch

Optional:
- wheat germ
- brown sugar
- plastic bag
- hammer

In 1895, Dr. John Kellogg partly cooked whole-wheat kernels, then rolled them flat and baked them until they were brown and dry. Seven years later, Kellogg invented corn flakes flavored with barley malt. Here are my experiments with making flakes. I used a flour-water mixture instead of whole-wheat kernels.

Method of Investigation

NOTE: Since you are using the stove, have an adult present.

1. In a small bowl, mix 1 tablespoon of wheat flour with 2½ tablespoons of water to make a thin batter.

2. Spread the batter evenly over a piece of aluminum foil.

3. Put in the toaster oven and broil until brown (about five minutes).

4. Let it cool and remove the foil by peeling it off the very large "flake." Turn the flake over and put it back in the toaster for about a minute and a half.

5. Break up into smaller flakes.

6. Repeat steps 1–5 using cornmeal instead of wheat flour, only add about ½ teaspoon cornstarch to the mixture so that it holds together.

Here's another recipe:

Grape Nuts® can also be made in your kitchen. Mix 1 cup of whole-wheat flour, ½ cup wheat germ, ¼ cup brown sugar, and 1 cup of water. Cover a cookie sheet with aluminum foil and spread the batter on the foil. Bake at 350°F for about one hour until it is brown. Let cool, then peel the foil off the very hard-baked "biscuit." Now you can see the problem of baking a flour-water mixture without any yeast or leavening agent. The result is a very hard product. So put your biscuit in a plastic bag and break it up with a hammer—ta da! Grape Nuts. The original cereal had to be soaked overnight in milk to make it edible. Yours won't be that hard.

Observations & Suggestions

How do your flakes compare to commercial flakes? Can you tell why some flakes are used as snack food and not cereal? Flakes that are made in oil are crispier and crunchier. Flakes that are baked are crisp but not as crunchy.

Key Words: John Harvey Kellogg • corn flakes

EXTRACT DNA IN YOUR KITCHEN

CHALLENGE LEVEL

MATERIALS AND EQUIPMENT

- knife
- onion
- blender
- measuring cup
- warm water
- measuring spoons
- salt
- small bowl
- colorless liquid soap (not detergent)
- toothpick
- small strainer
- coffee filter paper
- small glass custard cup
- meat tenderizer
- rubbing alcohol
- flashlight
- magnifier

Is it possible to see DNA for yourself without a fancy lab set up? You bet! In 1868, Friedrich Miescher (1844–1895), a Swiss biochemist, decided to study the nucleus of cells. Since he was a chemist, he attacked the problem of figuring out the nucleus by figuring out its chemistry. He extracted the nucleii from the pus cells found on the discarded bandages of wounded soldiers. Then he treated the nucleii with salt and acid. He obtained a material he called *nuclein*. Later it was renamed deoxyribonucleic acid or DNA for short. He was a man way ahead of his times because he could only guess that the nucleus of cells was important to heredity. In the next experiment you will extract DNA from cells in a process similar to the one Miescher used, but you'll be starting with an onion, not bandages. (What a relief!)

Method of Investigation

1. Peel and chop up the onion and put it in the blender with ¼ cup warm tap water and 1 teaspoon salt. Blend it for several seconds until it is fairly smooth in appearance.

   This mechanically breaks up the cell walls and draws the water out of them. The water must be warm because most biochemical processes speed up in warm water

2. Place the mixture in a small bowl. Add ¼ cup liquid soap. Mix for five minutes using a toothpick to prevent a lot of foam from forming.

   The cell membranes are made of lipids, a kind of fat. Soap reacts with lipids so that the lipids can be suspended in solution. You need to give the reaction enough time to occur, and you need to expose as much of the living material to the soap as possible.

3. Line a small strainer with coffee filter paper and set it over the custard cup. Put in the onion-salt-soap mixture. Let it drip for about ten minutes until you have at least 1 tablespoon in the cup.

   The filter paper will only let molecules through that are large enough to pass through the very small holes in the paper.

continued on next page ▶

Every science has its moment in the sun, when there is an explosion of ideas and a new technology starts to emerge. Biology's time began in the last decades of the twentieth century. The discovery of the structure and purpose of a single molecule that is found in every cell nucleus of every living thing paved the way. That molecule is called DNA. The building blocks of DNA are smaller molecules called *nucleotides*. There are only four different nucleotides, and the same four are found in every form of life. That sounds pretty simple, but wait. The order of the nucleotides as they link together is a code. Your DNA makes you a human being, a boy or a girl. It determines your looks, a large part of your intelligence and personality, certain diseases you may inherit, and it makes you related to your parents and siblings. And, in addition to containing the master plans for life, the DNA molecule can make perfect copies of itself. It is a molecule most worthy of study.

Most of the destroyed cells will remain behind.

4 Add ⅛ teaspoon of meat tenderizer to the liquid. Mix with a toothpick for about five minutes.

Meat tenderizer is an enzyme that breaks down proteins into amino acids. Since protein makes up most of the material inside cells, you are destroying the barrier of material surrounding the cell nucleii freeing up the DNA. Again, this reaction takes some time.

5 Slowly pour in some rubbing alcohol so that the amount of liquid is double what it was. The alcohol will form its own layer on top of the cell-debris mixture.

6 Shine a light down on the mixture and watch from the side. Strands of DNA will rise out of the cell debris up into the alcohol layer. If you stir gently, the strands will stick to each other. Let the experiment stand for several hours. Go back and check every once in a while to see what's happening to your DNA.

Observations & Suggestions

Alcohol is less dense than the mixture containing cellular debris and floats on top. DNA is more attracted to alcohol than it is to the cell debris mixture and will rise

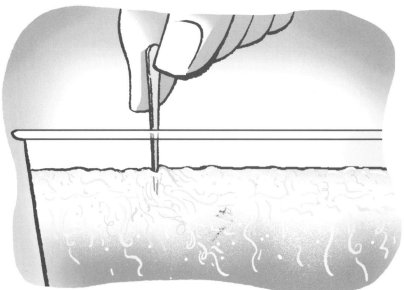

Here are two questions scientists asked about DNA, with the answers:

What is the job of DNA? To direct the synthesis of proteins. Proteins are made up of about twenty-four different amino acids that are like the letters of the alphabet. If the letters make up words, a protein is a paragraph. Each small sequence of nucleotides corresponds to a particular amino acid. So a chain of nucleotides is the master plan for a protein. The code for each protein is hidden in the nucleotide sequence.

How does DNA do its job? The secret lies in the structure of DNA. Most of the time, it is coiled up like a ball of yarn in the nucleus of cells. It makes up the small bodies in the nucleus known as genes which make up large bodies called chromosomes. DNA stretches out when it is involved in making a protein or when the cell is dividing. The shape of the DNA molecule was the object of an intense scientific study in the 1950s. Clues came from pictures taken with X rays, from chemistry and from physics. The model that was proposed was so beautiful and orderly that it stunned the world. DNA is like a rope ladder with solid rungs that has been twisted into a double spiral—a shape called a double helix. When DNA reproduces itself, it splits down the center of the rungs, and each strand builds up its mirror image. The model of DNA is named for two scientists who discovered it: James Watson and Francis Crick. They won a Nobel prize in 1962. It is called the Watson-Crick model.

through it. The tiny bubbles that are attached to the DNA threads are air bubbles that come out of the liquid and cling to the rough surface of DNA. These bubbles also help lift the DNA to the surface of the alcohol.

Notice how the tiny threads of DNA are attracted to each other. I found that after a while all the DNA was clumped together, floating on top of the alcohol. I lifted some of the threads out with a fork and looked at the tines of the fork with a small, inexpensive magnifier that

enlarges the image about thirty times. The fork tines were covered with tiny threads, like a spiderweb. The most amazing thing was that some of the DNA didn't clump together like a blob, but formed a spiral. The threads formed a twisted shape called a helix—an amazing clue to the shape of the molecule itself!

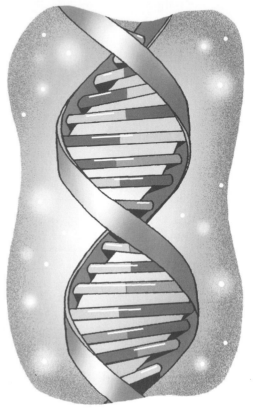

Key Words: DNA · protein synthesis · genetic code

LIGHT DESSERT

CHALLENGE LEVEL

MATERIALS
AND
EQUIPMENT

- an adult helper
- small bowl
- measuring cup
- 3 packages gelatin dessert:
  1 cherry (red)
  1 blueberry (blue)
  1 lime (green)
- 3 small plastic containers from the supermarket deli department (about 4½ inches in diameter)
- refrigerator
- red light pointer laser from stationery store (Note: These are fairly inexpensive. Do not shine into anyone's eyes!)
- white plate
- knife
- spatula
- a flashlight that can be focused

Would you believe that a gelatin dessert can show how light travels through colored filters and how it can be internally reflected?

Method of Investigation

NOTE: Since you will be using the stove, have an adult helper.

1. Make the three desserts. In a small bowl, mix 1 cup of boiling water with each package of gelatin dessert mix. Pour each color into its own deli container. Be sure to wash out the bowl before mixing the next dessert. Let the desserts set several hours in the refrigerator to make sure they are firmly gelled.

2. Shine the laser through the side of each color gelatin dessert. In which color does the beam shine through all the way? Which has the shortest transmission of the beam?

3. Loosen the red gelatin dessert by setting the container in hot water for about one minute. (Be careful not to let the water directly touch the gelatin.) Turn a plate upside down on top of the container with the

gelatin. Invert the gelatin container and the plate. Holding both the plate and the plastic container, shake a few times so the gelatin lands on the plate.

4 With a long sharp knife, cut the unmolded red gelatin in half so that it forms two D shapes. With a spatula, return one D shape back to the container.

5 Shine the laser beam horizontally into the gelatin perpendicular to the straight edge of the D. Look down from the top as you move the laser from near the top edge down toward the center. You will see the beam pass through the red gelatin, strike the curved surface, and bounce across the curved surface until it hits it again. If the angle is right, you will see the beam make two bends before it leaves the gelatin. At the right angle the edge of the gelatin acts like a mirror and reflects

the laser beam internally. At other angles the edge of the gelatin is like a window and the beam passes right throught it.

6 Shine the laser through the red gelatin perpendicular to the straight edge of the D, while you hold up a white sheet of paper vertically so that the emerging beam can strike it. When it reaches a certain angle, however, it will not emerge, but will reflect internally. This critical angle varies according to the medium the beam is traveling through and the color of the beam.

7 Try the experiment again using a flashlight with a beam that can be focused. Can you see internal reflection with ordinary light?

Observations & Suggestions

Red gelatin (which is transparent) transmits the red wavelengths of light. All other colors are absorbed. Since the laser is also red, red gelatin transmits this light. The tiny particles of gelatin act like tiny mirrors and reflect the laser light so that you see the beam as it travels through the gelatin.

continued on next page ▶

Blueberry gelatin is a color called cyan. Lime gelatin is green. The colors of the rainbow, which are all the visible colors, are ordered red, orange, yellow, green, blue, indigo, violet. You can remember this sequence as ROY G BIV. The laser will travel farther in the green gelatin than it will in the cyan, where it is almost completely absorbed.

You can see how a glass baking dish can internally reflect a beam. Shine your laser (or flashlight) directly down one side of a baking dish. Look at the opposite edge to see where the beam of light emerges. Notice the size of the emerging beam compared to the size of the emerging flashlight beam. It is in the nature of a laser beam to not spread out like ordinary light.

Here are some other fun things to do with your laser:

See how far it travels at night. (Laser beams don't diverge. All the light is traveling in the same direction.)

Shine it on a stop sign at night. (All of the laser light is reflected back toward you so you get an enhanced effect. It's amazing what the reflectors can do to a laser).

Shine it down at a glass coffee table. See two points of light on the wall as the beam reflects off both the top and bottom surface of the glass. Vary the angle of the laser to change the distance between the two spots.

Rotate the laser as you shine it through one lens of a pair of polarized, UV-protected sunglasses. If the laser light gets dimmer until it almost disappears, you know that your laser is made up of polarized light.

Key Words: total internal reflection • laser

PLAYING WITH PLASTIC

Making Coasters from Cups (pg. 63) • Plastic Wraps (pg. 65)

Plastics are made from small molecules called *hydrocarbons* found in petroleum. Many small hydrocarbons connect chemically to form chains called *polymers*. Different polymers have different properties and are used for different kinds of packaging. PET (polyethylene terephthalate) is used for soft drink bottles. HDPE (high density polyethylene) is used in milk, juice, and laundry product bottles. Vinyl (polyvinyl chloride or PVC) is used for shrink wrap and for some cooking oil and water bottles. LDPE (low density polyethylene) is used for grocery bags, or in ice cream tubs. PP (polypropylene) is used for some yogurt cups and ketchup bottles. PS (polystyrene) is used for yogurt cups, clear berry boxes, and all foamed polystyrene items, such as Styrofoam®. You can tell what a plastic item is made from by looking for the letters just below the triangle of arrows that tells you the item is recyclable.

MAKING COASTERS FROM CUPS

CHALLENGE LEVEL

Would you believe that some plastic yogurt cups were once flat as cookies? When it comes to packaging materials for food products, it's hard to beat plastic. It's cheap, it's strong and lightweight, it protects food without interacting with it, and it can be recycled.

How were plastic cups made? Heat reveals the past of a PS plastic cup.

Method of Investigation

NOTE: Since you will be using the oven, have an adult present when you do this experiment.

1. Preheat the oven to 450°F.

2. Place a clean yogurt cup, right side up, in the center of a cookie sheet.

continued on next page ▶

MATERIALS AND EQUIPMENT

- an adult helper
- an oven with a window in it (a toaster oven will work)
- yogurt cups marked with a PS on the bottom just below the triangle that says they're recyclable
- a cookie sheet
- a spatula
- Styrofoam cups
- Styrofoam trays from the meat department of your supermarket. If you tell the butcher that you're doing a science project, he'll probably give you some for nothing.

3. Place in the oven so that you can watch it through the oven door. Let the cup cook for about five minutes. It will melt and become a flat circle.

4. When it is completely melted, remove it from the oven, let it cool, and take it off the cookie sheet with a spatula.

5. Lower the oven temperature to 250°F and watch a Styrofoam® cup melt. Watch the trays from the meat department melt.

Yogurt cups are manufactured from flat sheets of polystyrene that are placed over a hot mold. Pieces called plugs push up on the sheet. High pressure air on one side of the mold and a vacuum on the other also help shape the plastic. After the molded polystyrene has cooled, the many yogurt cups are cut apart. You can see the sharp edges of the cut on the "coaster" you made. The finished cups are then printed on with graphics about the product.

Yogurt cup manufacturers can test the strength of a cup by remelting it, called diagnostic shrinking. If the stress is evenly distributed by the mold, that means the cup is well made or strong. A well-made cup flattens into a circle when it is reheated. If the stress is uneven, the reheated cup will not form a flat circle

Observations & Suggestions

Polystyrene, the plastic that styrofoam is made of, is a thermoplastic with a memory. When you heat it, it returns to the flat sheet it was before it became a yogurt cup. The temperature at which polystyrene becomes most flexible is about 400°F but it will become distorted slightly above the temperature of boiling water.

If you heat PET (sometimes called PETE) it will melt a little bit but it will also turn white. This is because it forms crystals as the plastic combines with oxygen in the air. This also happens when you leave it in the sun. Ultraviolet light also causes the plastic to crystallize.

Key Words: polystyrene · history of plastics

PLASTIC WRAPS

CHALLENGE LEVEL

MATERIALS AND EQUIPMENT

- ½ onion
- 2 or 3 different kinds of plastic wrap
- fabric softener sheets
- pen
- tape measure

How well does plastic wrap protect food? Wraps are thin films of plastic. They are made in two ways. Melted plastic can be squeezed through a slit so that it comes out the other side as a thin film. Melted plastic can also be blown into a large bubble. Then the air is let out of the bubble, leaving behind a double layer of plastic film.

Not all plastic films are made of the same kind of plastic. Some plastic wraps are like glass. No air or water can pass through them. Others are like chain-link fences. Both moisture and water can pass through. See which is which in the next experiment.

Method of Investigation

Does plastic film seal off odors?

1. Wrap a piece of cut onion in different kinds of plastic wrap. Wait about a half an hour until all the onion odor has cleared from the air. Sniff the different wrapped onions. You will be able to smell onion through the plastic wraps that let air and water pass through them.

What makes plastic wrap cling?

2. Look for things that "kill" the cling. Try and get plastic wrap to cling to different surfaces. Will it cling to wood, leather, metal, glass, and other plastic? Do you think there is any static involved with the cling? Spray some wrap with antistatic fabric softener or wipe it with an antistatic fabric softener sheet. Does it still cling? Pull it off a roll and let it sit for a day before you try and get it to cling. Will it still cling?

How stretchable is the film?

3. Compare the "draw" strengths of different plastic wraps. Poke the rounded back end of a pen into a square of wrap, so that the wrap stretches as you push the pen. Measure approximately how far you can push the pen before the wrap tears. There are a number of factors that affect the "draw": the smoothness of the pen (metal pen cases work better than plastic), the nature of the wrap, the shape of the pen case (if it's too pointed it will tear sooner) and the force you use—move very slowly.

Key Words: plastic film · plastic wraps

CHAPTER 3

Inspirations from the Toy Store

Ever feel like you're in another world when you play with your toys? You are so involved with you own imagination that you don't hear the call to dinner. The best thing about play is that you make up all the rules. You can try stuff out just for fun, just because you thought of it.

Believe it or not, the best science is just like play. It is thinking about what you observe and then trying to guess what changes you can make in those things. Sometimes when you make a change something unexpected happens and you make a discovery.

Modern science began when a great scientist, Galileo Galilei (1564–1642), an Italian professor of mathematics, thought long and hard about how balls roll. Since a ball is sometimes called the "universal toy," this chapter starts with balls and uses lots of other toys as the inspiration for many science projects.

BOUNCING

CHALLENGE LEVEL

How can you tell a great ball from a dead one? You can have a bouncing contest with different kinds of balls. If you like math, you can do some measurements and calculations and put a number on the best bouncer.

Method of Investigation

1. Tape a column made from sheets of paper to a wall from the ground to just over 6 feet high.

2. Use the marker to make a horizontal line 6 feet from the ground. Make marks for each foot under 6 feet. You can also mark off ½-foot lines if you wish.

3. Have your friend hold a ball at the 6-foot mark and drop it. See how high it bounces. This is called the "bounce-back." It may take several trials until you get consistent readings for the height of the bounce-back.

4. Repeat this procedure with other balls. No ball will bounce higher than the 6-foot starting point, but some will come closer to the starting point than others.

Observations & Suggestions

Rubber is a material that has a memory. If you distort it by stretching, twisting, or compressing, it returns to its original shape after the force is removed. Some energy is used to restore the rubber to its original shape. The collision with the floor compresses a rubber ball momentarily. Its return to its original shape is part of the force going into the bounce-back.

How does temperature affect the bounce-back? Put balls in the freezer for several hours. Compare their

After you have made your measurements, do the math. The bounce-back height of the ball will be some percentage of the original height. The formula for finding the bounce-back (B-B) is:

$$B\text{-}B = \frac{\text{height after bounce}}{\text{initial height (6 feet)}} \times 100$$

So if a ball bounces to a height of 4 feet its bounce-back is 66%.

There is a law in science called the "conservation of energy," which states that energy cannot be lost, only transformed. If a ball bounced perfectly, its bounce-back would be exactly as high as its initial position when it was dropped. Since it doesn't, according to the law the energy had to go someplace. Perhaps the rubber of the ball absorbed some of the energy as heat. Perhaps the floor absorbed some of the energy. Perhaps some of the energy is transferred into sound. In any case, some energy is transformed into heat energy with each bounce until there is no energy of motion left.

bounce to similar balls that are at room temperature.

Another way of measuring bouncing is to count the number of bounces a ball makes until it stops after you drop it. My Superball bounced about seventeen times before it fluttered to the ground. You might compare the number of bounces to the bounce-back percentages to see if there is a connection.

Put a tennis ball on top of a basketball and drop them together from a height of about 4 feet. Watch out as the tennis ball shoots

into the air, much higher than the basketball bounces. In this case the small ball is still falling when the larger ball bounces up to meet it. The force of the collision is

enough to add a lot of energy to the small ball so that it leaves the impact with increased velocity.

What effect do different kinds of floors have on bounce-back? Many sports are played on different surfaces. Tennis, for example, is played on clay, grass, and a rubberized concrete. Why aren't basketball courts covered with carpet? What happens if you drop a Superball into a container of sand? Some materials absorb more energy than others. What kind of flooring will give you the greatest bounce-back?

ROLLING

MATERIALS AND EQUIPMENT

- 8 sections of Hot Wheels® tracks
- tape
- a coffee table or other piece of furniture
- a heavy book
- an assortment of balls, large, small, hollow, solid
- a ruler
- a scissors
- an empty film canister

How fast do things fall? Can you find out without a watch? For thousands of years people believed that objects fell to the ground because that was their natural place. They also believed that heavier things fall faster than lighter ones. Galileo Galilei became the father of modern science when he rolled balls in his laboratory. You, too, can discover what he discovered.

Method of Investigation

1. Make two separate runways by connecting four Hot Wheels tracks together. Lay them out side by side.

2. Raise one end of both tracks about 18 inches (I attached mine to a coffee table) and tape them in place against some furniture.

3. Place a heavy book to act as a barrier across the track at the bottom of the slope.

4. Place a ball in each of the tracks at the elevated end and hold them in place by resting them against a ruler held horizontally across both tracks. When you remove the ruler, you simultaneously release both balls to roll down the track. They are stopped by the book at the bottom of the slope. By listening for the collision, you can tell which ball arrived first or if they arrived at the same time. Do several trials with each set of balls to make sure of your results.

5. Move the barrier to the end of the track and race the balls.

6. Compare a large ball and a very small one; a tennis ball and a smooth ball; a solid rubber ball and a hollow Ping-Pong® ball.

7 Use a pair of scissors to cut down a film canister to make a 1-inch cylinder. Have a race between the cylinder and a ball.

Observations & Suggestions

You have just repeated Galileo's breakthrough experiment. Although you might see one ball reach the wood at the bottom of the slope a split second before the other, repeated experiments should show you that the balls arrive pretty much simultaneously. Galileo's experiments led him to formulate the first law of motion: an object in motion tends to remain in motion and an object at rest tends to remain at rest

unless it is acted upon by an external force. The force of gravity pulls the balls down the ramp. The forces that might slow one ball more than another are friction between the ball and the ramp and air resistance.

In the race between the cylinder and the ball, the cylinder might be slowed down slightly because there is more contact between the cylinder surface and the track than the ball and the track. But the difference will still be too small to create a large effect as they roll down the incline. Let's assume that they are tied neck and neck when they come to the bottom of the incline. A new race now begins on the flat.

The ball will win because it is solid. Rolling speed depends on how close the weight is to the center of the rolling object. The weight of the ball is closer to the center than the weight of the cylinder which is hollow. As a result, the solid ball rolls faster than the hollow cylinder. Try the experiment again, comparing a hollow Ping-Pong® ball and a hollow cylinder. Since both are hollow, the weight distribution around the center is pretty much the same. There is probably less friction for the ball than the cylinder, which might give it a slight edge.

Try this experiment again, changing the steepness of the slope.

Legend says that Galileo dropped a heavy ball and a light one off a balcony on the Tower of Pisa. The balls landed at the same time, proving that the mass of an object did not affect the acceleration of gravity pulling the balls toward a collision with the earth. This story may or may not be true. We do know, however, that Galileo was fascinated by falling objects. Their speed seemed to continually increase as they fell. In the early seventeenth century there was no clock yet invented that could time the rapid descent of a falling body. So Galileo correctly figured that he could "dilute" gravity by rolling balls down a ramp. He assumed that the *rate* of increase in speed of a rolling object would be the same as it would have falling, although the object would be traveling much more slowly. The closer the angle of the ramp was to vertical, the closer the acceleration would be to the actual acceleration of gravity. Galileo's ramps had a low incline and he could time the distance traveled by the balls with a water clock—a timing device that had regular drips of water.

Key Words: laws of motion · acceleration of gravity · Galileo Galilei

SPINNING

Straw and Lid Tops (pg. 72) • An Unbalanced Ping-Pong® Ball (pg. 74)

There is something quite magical about a top. Left alone it will rest forever with its rim and its point both touching the ground. But if you give it a spin, it will stand up on its point, perfectly balanced, until friction between the point and the ground erodes its speed and it begins to wobble and roam until it tips over and stops.

In addition to its spin, most tops also show a kind of motion called *precession*. The top axis of a top traces out a circular path in the air. Tops also show some personality in the way that they spin. Some tops settle down to a long stable spin, others wander about, some spin a long time, others quickly die out. Make your own study of the various things that affect the way a simple finger spin top works.

STRAW AND LID TOPS

CHALLENGE LEVEL

MATERIALS AND EQUIPMENT

- scissors
- small diameter (1/2 inch) plastic 5-inch long straws
- nail
- plastic coffee lids with a symmetrical pattern (used to snap on Styrofoam® cups for take-out coffee)
- stopwatch
- glue

What goes into the design of a great top? You can have a spinning contest with the simplest and most inexpensive (free) top imaginable!

Method of Investigation

1. Cut a straw in half to make a stem (the axis of rotation) for your top. Hold one end of the straw tightly between your thumb and index finger. As you push your thumb forward and your index finger backward, you put a spin on the straw. Try and spin the straw so that it stands on its end. (No way!)

2. To make a top, you need some weight around the axis of rotation. Use a nail to start a hole in the center of a coffee cup lid (Some may already have a tiny hole near the center. Ignore this hole and start your own). Push the nail in to enlarge the hole so that you can just push the straw into it and

the straw will be firmly fixed wherever you stop pushing it. To start, have the straw stick out of the bottom about ½ inch with most of the straw above the lid. Now try and spin it.

3 Have a friend use a stopwatch to time the spins. Do this at least five times and take an average.

4 Push the stem in a little further and spin the top. This top will fall sooner, but it will continue to roll around its axis for a while. How does the total spinning time, including the rolling, compare with the top where the lid is closer to the ground?

5 Change the distribution of weight around the axis. Cut off the outer lip of a lid and spin it.

6 Add weight by putting glue around the outer rim on one lid; on another, fill in the inner pattern with glue; add glue to the center indentation on yet another (be sure to put the straw axis in place before the glue dries). Keep a record of a spinning contest with all these various tops.

Observations & Suggestions

In general, you will find that the closer the lid is placed to the tabletop, the longer the top will spin. As the lid moves up the axis, the faster you need to spin the top to keep it balanced. As you add weight (the glue) toward the center, the faster the top will spin.

As long as a top is spinning, it has a stability that allows it to balance on a point. The spinning gives it something called *angular momentum* that can work as a force against gravity. A spinning bicycle wheel allows you to balance on its rim as long as the wheel is spinning. When you stop, gravity takes over and the bike cannot remain upright. This resistance of a spinning object to a change in its orientation is used in a gyroscope. A gyroscope is a top that spins in a framework that is free to move without changing the direction of the axis of the spinning gyroscope. A compass mounted on a gyroscope on a ship always keeps the compass level, even as the ship gets tossed about by waves. An electric motor keeps the spin going against friction. Gyroscopes are also used in the Hubble Space Telescope to keep it pointed toward the stars it's observing.

Key Words: angular momentum · spinning tops · gyroscopes

AN UNBALANCED PING-PONG® BALL

CHALLENGE LEVEL

MATERIALS AND EQUIPMENT

MATERIALS AND EQUIPMENT

- a Ping-Pong ball
- a small sharp-pointed nail
- sink with stopper
- flashlight
- egg carton or ice-cube tray
- freezer
- waterproof marker

Can you make a top spin upside down? Ever seen a top that looks like half a solid ball on a stem? When you spin it on the round side it turns over and winds up spinning on its stem. The top-heavy side rises against gravity. You can make your own version of this top with ingenuity and a Ping-Pong ball.

Method of Investigation

1. Position the ball so that the seam is the equator. Make a small hole with the nail at the north pole.

2. Plug the sink and fill it with water. Submerge the Ping-Pong ball under water with the hole near the top. Very gently press on the side of the ball and release. Bubbles will emerge from the hole as air goes out. Water is replacing the air.

3. Repeat this several times, occasionally removing the ball and holding it in front of a flashlight with the equator of the ball horizontal. You want to fill the ball halfway so that the water level is at the equator.

1. 2. 3. 4. 5. 6.

4 Set the half-filled ball in the egg container or ice cube tray with the north pole up. Put in the freezer.

5 Remove the frozen ball and wipe it dry. Color the southern hemisphere of the ball with a waterproof marker.

6 Place the ball on a table with the colored side down. Hold the thumb of one hand horizontally across the ball's equator while you hold the middle finger of the other hand on the other side of the ball. Put a spin on the ball by moving your fingers apart in opposite directions. It may take a few practice tries to get the knack.

Observations & Suggestions

Watch as the colored hemisphere, containing the ice, rises and the ball spins on the hollow side. The heavier side rises to the top! It takes some hard thinking to figure out why this happens.

If an object is free to spin in any direction, it will spin around a central point that is the focus of all its weight. This point is called its *center of gravity*. A sphere's center of gravity is its geometrical center, even if the ball is hollow. When you fill the ball halfway with water, the water lowers the center of gravity below the equator. An unstable object will come to rest so that its center of gravity is as low as possible. Since a ball can roll, the ice-filled (or water-filled) hemisphere will be on the bottom when the ball is at rest. Spinning, however, puts a force on the ball that works against gravity so that it tends to resist any change in the direction of its axis. Since a top's axis is vertical, the spinning top is balanced when it is on its point. (A bicycle's axis is horizontal so the wheel stays balanced on its rim.) In the case of the weighted ball, the force from the spin raises the center of gravity above the equator and the new point of contact becomes the south pole. As the spin deteriorates, the center of gravity again falls toward the earth.

Key Words: center of gravity · angular momentum · spinning and center of gravity

IDENTIFIABLE FLYING OBJECTS

Getting to Know Bernoulli (pg. 76) • The Flying Cuff (pg. 78) •
Paper Airplane (pg. 79)

Violent storms like tornadoes and hurricanes leave very little doubt that the wind can make things fly through the air. Wind is matter. Matter striking other things creates a force, and a force can move other objects. The surprising thing about moving air, however, is the *direction* of the force it creates. Properly applied, moving air can create *lift*, a force acting in a direction opposite to gravity, and can keep heavier-than-air objects from falling to earth. Discover some of the principles of lift in the next set of experiments.

CHALLENGE LEVEL

GETTING TO KNOW BERNOULLI

MATERIALS AND EQUIPMENT

- scissors
- a sheet of standard white paper
- funnel
- Ping-Pong® ball

How can the direction of wind make things fly?

Part 1
Method of Investigation

Cut a 1-inch-by-11-inch-wide strip of paper from a piece of typing paper. With your index finger, hold the strip against your chin with the paper hanging down over your finger. Blow down on the top surface of the paper. Amazingly, the paper rises, becoming horizontal as long as you keep blowing.

Observations & Suggestions

When you blow across on the surface of the paper, the air pressure on that surface decreases. Since the air on the other side of the paper is not moving, its pressure is greater and it pushes the paper up. The minute you stop blowing, the pressure on both sides of the paper equalizes and the paper falls again.

Part 2
Method of Investigation

Put a Ping-Pong® ball into a medium-sized funnel. There is no way that you can blow the ball out of the funnel by holding it vertically and blowing up from the bottom. However, if you put the edge of the funnel just under your lower lip and blow horizontally across the top of the funnel, the ball will pop right out.

Observations & Suggestions

As you blow up from the bottom of the funnel, air rushes around the sides of the Ping-Pong ball. The air pressure on the sides of the ball becomes less than the air pressure from the still air pushing down on the ball. The harder you blow, the more firmly the ball will sit in the funnel. However, when you blow horizontally across the top of the funnel, the vertical air pressure decreases. The air under the ball now has the greater pressure (because it is not moving) and will force the ball up and out of the funnel.

Daniel Bernoulli (1700–1782) was a Swiss mathematician who became interested in the force exerted by moving gases. Bernoulli's principle states that as a gas moves horizontally across a surface, the vertical pressure of the gas on the surface decreases. The faster the gas moves, the less the air pressure at right angles to the gas's motion. An airplane wing is designed to take advantage of Bernoulli's principle. The top of the wing is curved. As the plane moves forward, air traveling over the top of the wing moves faster than air under the wing. As a result, the air under the wing has greater air pressure than the air on top and the plane gets a lift.

Key Words: Bernoulli's principle

THE FLYING CUFF

MATERIALS AND EQUIPMENT

- **a sheet of standard white paper**
- **scissors**
- **tape**

Can flying objects have unusual shapes and still fly? Here's an amazing wingless wonder.

Method of Investigation

1 Fold the upper-left-hand corner of the paper toward you so that the top edge is exactly on top of the right edge. Crease the paper.

2 Cut off the extra paper below the double sheet. This will leave you with a square that has been folded in half diagonally.

3 Open the square and turn it so that the crease runs from left to right. Make a ¼-inch fold on the corner on the bottom. Keep folding the bottom edge over and over again until your "cuff" just covers the crease.

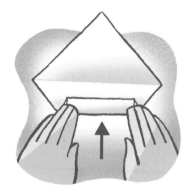

4 Keep your folded band on the outside and curve the paper. Slip one pointed end of the "cuff" into the other point. Fasten the ends together with tape. You have made a folded cuff with a tail.

5 Throw your flying cuff with the cuff in front and the tail in the rear.

Observations & Suggestions

I got some very long glides by throwing the cuff gently off the palm of my hand. What happens when you bend the tail up or down? Compare your gliders to some paper airplanes.

Key Words: paper airplanes

PAPER AIRPLANE

CHALLENGE LEVEL

MATERIALS
AND
EQUIPMENT

- a sheet of standard white paper

D o you enjoy making paper airplanes? There are lots of designs in other books. This is one of the best. It really glides.

Method of Investigation

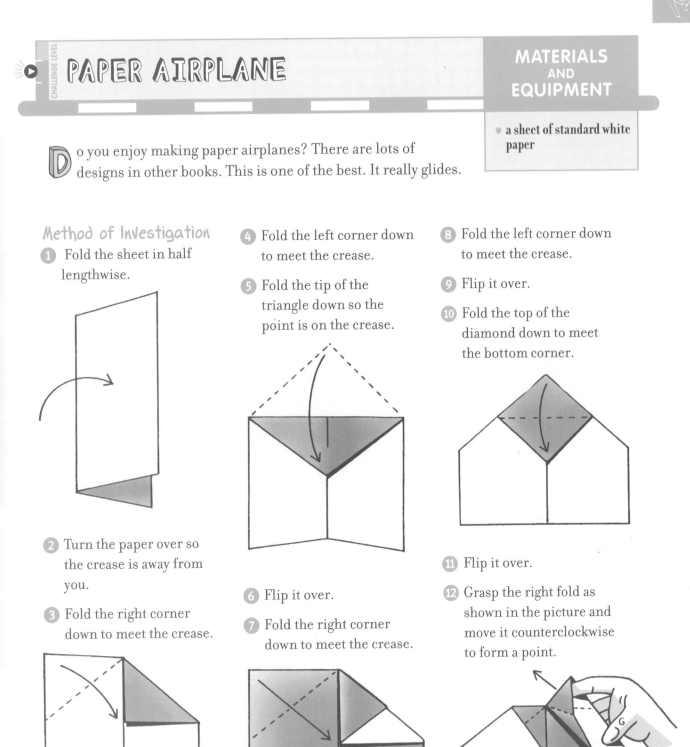

1 Fold the sheet in half lengthwise.

2 Turn the paper over so the crease is away from you.

3 Fold the right corner down to meet the crease.

4 Fold the left corner down to meet the crease.

5 Fold the tip of the triangle down so the point is on the crease.

6 Flip it over.

7 Fold the right corner down to meet the crease.

8 Fold the left corner down to meet the crease.

9 Flip it over.

10 Fold the top of the diamond down to meet the bottom corner.

11 Flip it over.

12 Grasp the right fold as shown in the picture and move it counterclockwise to form a point.

continued on next page ▶

13 Repeat with the left fold.

14 Your initial fold is now the V of the center of your plane. Make accordion folds as shown in the picture.

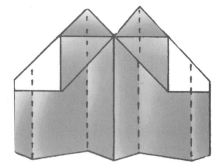

15 Hold from the V at the bottom and release at the end of your throw.

Observations & Suggestions

The key to a great paper airplane is the location of its center of gravity, its stability in the air and its lift, which only occurs when the plane is moving forward. You can change a glider's center of gravity by putting a paper clip on the "V" under the nose and adjusting how far forward or backward the clip is. Friction between the plane and the air is called *drag*. Without an engine to constantly propel it forward, drag eventually slows down the plane so that it ends up on the ground. Properly thrown, this airplane will stay up for several seconds and glide gently to a landing. To make it turn, tilt it one way or the other as you throw it. For a challenging project, compare this plane to other paper airplane designs.

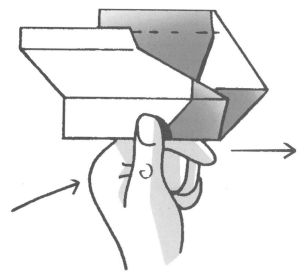

Key Words: paper airplanes · principles of flight

PLAYING WITH SOUND

The Slinky Model of a Sound Wave (pg. 81) · Talk Under Water (pg. 82) · The Sound of Silence (pg. 83)

Sound is energy traveling in waves through matter. Sound travels through air, water, wood, even the bones of your head. If there is no matter, there is no sound. In space, for instance, there is no sound.

CHALLENGE LEVEL

THE SLINKY® MODEL OF A SOUND WAVE

MATERIALS AND EQUIPMENT

- a metal Slinky
- a friend

Can you imagine what a sound wave looks like? A Slinky can give you a good idea.

Method of Investigation

1. You take one end of the Slinky and your friend takes the other end. Stretch the Slinky across the room.

2. One of you pinches six Slinky coils together and lets go. Watch as the wave travels down the Slinky and bounces back from the end. (An echo is bouncing sound waves.)

3. See if you and your friend can start a wave at the same time. Watch what happens when the waves meet.

Observations & Suggestions

When you pinch the coils together, you set up an area of compression next to an area of spreading out, or *rarefaction.*

The areas of compression and rarefaction travel down the length of the spring as the individual coils vibrate back and forth.

Try setting up a wave by holding one end of the Slinky and doing a quick push-pull motion.

While the Slinky is stretched out, hold your end with just your fingertips. You want to secure the spring with the smallest amount of contact. With your other hand, flick your middle finger on the end coil. Hold it up to your ear as you flick your finger. You set up a wave, and you can hear it ping through the spring.

Key Words: Slinky · sound waves

TALK UNDER WATER

MATERIALS AND EQUIPMENT

- 2 empty tennis ball cans
- a friend
- a swimming pool

Have you ever wanted to speak to an underwater friend? While searching for ideas in a toy store, I found a fun gadget that allows you to speak to your friends when you are underwater. Naturally, we had a lot of fun testing it out. The basic idea is to have a device that puts air with sound in it underwater so that the underwater listener can hear it. The toy is designed so that the speaker as well as the listener can be underwater. You don't need the toy, however, if the speaker stays on the surface. An empty tennis ball can works just fine.

Method of Investigation

1. Hold an upright tennis ball can so that most of it is underwater but no water can get into it.

2. Practice speaking into the can by putting your mouth right up to it.

3. Have your friend go underwater while you speak into the partially submerged can. Did your friend get the message?

Observations & Suggestions

How did your voice sound underwater? Was it higher or lower? How far can the swimmer be and still get the message?

Sound travels in air at a speed of about 754 miles per hour, but it travels almost five times faster in seawater. Sound is used underwater to map the ocean floor, to find fish, and to detect enemy submarines. Sonar is the detection system. Sound waves are sent out and an echo means that the wave has struck something. The speed with which an echo returns is a measure of where an object is located.

Key Words: sound · speed of sound · Water Talkies®

CHALLENGE LEVEL

THE SOUND OF SILENCE

MATERIALS AND EQUIPMENT

- 2 packages of plastic straws (soda size)
- rubber bands

Since sound is a wave that passes through matter, in a vacuum, where there are no molecules, there would be no sound. What does that silence sound like? In the next experiment, you make a device that limits the motion of air and as a result cuts off sound.

Method of Investigation

1 Remove the straws from one of the packages and hold them all together. Rest one end on a tabletop so that all the ends line up.

2 Put rubber bands around the pack of straws. The end should look like a honeycomb.

3 Make a similar pack with the straws from the other package.

4 Put the ends of one pack of straws against your ear. Listen through them. Put your hand over the open end to completely block them off. You are now experiencing "dead" air.

5 Cover both ears with packs of straws and cover the ends. This is what silence sounds like.

Observations & Suggestions

Can you hear anything through the straws when the ends are open to the environment? When you cover the ends, you are preventing sound from entering the straws. Since you are not generating much sound from your ears, you are listening to columns of dead air. When you listen to a seashell, you hear the echos of sound from the environment as well as sound from your ear touching the shell. But in this case, there is not likely to be any echoes.

Most sound-insulating material has pockets of air in a substance that is able to absorb sound without sending off an echo. Experiment with different sizes of straws.

MAGIC SAND®

MATERIALS AND EQUIPMENT

- an adult helper
- measuring cup
- clean sand (the kind that's used for sand painting)
- a shallow box lid
- silicone spray or lubricant
- 2 or 3 small containers (I used custard cups)
- water
- more clean sand (the kind that's used for sand painting)
- commercial Magic Sand or make your own from clean sand (the kind that's used for sand painting)
- spoon

Does water always make things wet? When water is attracted to a surface, the surface gets wet. But when water is not attracted, the surface stays dry. It doesn't happen very often, and when it does, it's fun to play with. You can buy Magic Sand at toy and novelty stores. But you can also make your own.

Method of Investigation

NOTE: Do this experiment outside with an adult present.

1. Spread about a cup of clean sand in a box lid. Spray it with silicone spray or lubricant. Do not inhale the spray. Shake the sand around and spray it again. Let it dry overnight.

2. Fill a small dish ¾ full of water. Sprinkle your homemade treated sand onto the water's surface so that it becomes coated. If you sprinkle gently, most of the sand will stay on the surface and not sink to the bottom.

3. Repeat step 2 with untreated sand and with commercial Magic Sand if you have it.

4. Gently push your fingertip down on the surface of the treated sand. You can push all the way to the bottom of the dish. Remove your finger. Ta da! It's dry!

5 Repeat step 4 with the untreated sand. Do you get the same results?

6 In two clean dishes of water, put a spoonful of each of the sands. Stir. Notice that the treated sand stays in one clump and the untreated sand mixes with water. Bring up some of the submerged treated sand on the spoon. Feel it. Do the same with the untreated sand.

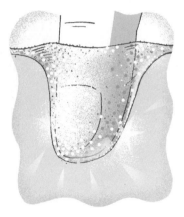

Observations & Suggestions

When you sprinkled treated sand on the surface of the water, the water tension held it up. The layer of treated sand was a barrier between your finger and the water, keeping your finger from getting wet. When you pushed down on the surface, you stretched the water's surface, but as long as you didn't break through, the sand kept you dry.

You might notice a silvery light next to the sand when it is underwater. This is due to a thin layer of air that is next to the dry sand. When light passes through the water to this thin layer of air, it is bent or refracted. You see it as a silvery layer.

A water molecule has an imbalance in the way its electrical charge is distributed. One end is more positively charged and the other more negatively charged. Most surfaces also contain molecules with charges on them. As a result, water molecules are attracted to these surfaces and stick to them or wet them. The silicone spray you used contains silicone—a compound that is very *hydrophobic*, or "water-fearing." Silicone's electrical charges aren't separated, so the water molecules aren't attracted to it at all. Water molecules are also attracted to each other. This attraction allows wet sand to stick to other wet sand and it puts a skin on the surface of water called *surface tension*.

Most surfaces also have molecules with a charge separation. The oppositely charged ends of the water and surface molecules attract each other and the water sticks to, or wets, the surface.

Key Words: Magic Sand · water repellents · hydrophobic

WATER LOVERS

CHALLENGE LEVEL

- measuring cups
- 1 gallon of distilled water (don't get mineral water)
- 3 or 4 bowls
- measuring spoons
- salt
- labels
- pen or pencil
- ruler
- scale (optional)
- paper
- 3 or 4 identical "grow creatures" (I used alligators) from a toy store or Soil Moist spikes (from a garden store)
- several granules of Soil Moist (optional)

What can you do with materials that absorb water? If you want to thicken gravy, you mix a starch, like flour, in water and add it to the gravy. Starch is a polymer that is *hydrophilic*, or "water-loving." In recent years science has come up with plastic water-loving polymers. They are used to make Soil Moist™, contact lenses, and "grow creatures" that expand enormously when you put them in water. Salt changes the ability of this plastic to absorb water. See for yourself.

Method of Investigation

1. First prepare your salt solutions. Pour 3 cups of distilled water into one of the bowls. Put 3 cups of distilled water and ½ teaspoon salt in a second bowl. This solution is 0.2% salt. In a third bowl put 3 cups of water and 2 teaspoons of salt. This is an 0.8% solution. If you wish to make a fourth bowl, put 3½ teaspoons of salt in 3 cups of distilled water to make a 1.4% solution. Label all the bowls.

2. Measure the length of your grow creature. (You can also weigh it.) Record your measurements. Put an identical grow creature or Soil Moist spike in each bowl. You can also put in about five Soil Moist granules.

3. Soak the plastics in the solutions overnight. Measure and weigh the objects the next day.

Observations & Suggestions

Grow creatures are made of a plastic called polyacrylate. It contains many negatively charged areas. Since water molecules also have negative and positive areas, they are attracted to the plastic. Part of the expansion of the gel is due to the moving away from each other of the negatively charged areas. The plastic also has an internal cell-like framework that swells as water is trapped. Water fills the space created in a network of stretched polyacrylate molecules.

When salt is added to water, it splits into positively charged sodium ions and negatively charged chlorine ions. (An ion is a charged particle.) The sodium is attracted to the negatively charged poly-acrylate areas, competing with the water. If a sodium ion attaches to a negative spot, no water will go there. As a result, the polymer absorbs a lot less water when salt is present. You might also want to see what effect other solutions have on the absorbency of a hydrophilic polymer. Put grow creatures into undiluted vinegar, which is a 5% acid solution, a baking soda solution (1 teaspoon in 3 cups of water), which will be 5%, undiluted rubbing alcohol, which is a 70% solution, etc. Try mineral water and tap water.

Polyacrylate is in disposable diapers. Pour water from a measuring cup onto a diaper. Tilt the diaper back and forth. Keep adding water until it is completely saturated. How many cups did it take? Compare different brands of diapers. Dissect a diaper you've poured water on. Look for the swollen granules of polyacrylate.

Soil Moist™ is made of another hydrophilic polymer called polyacrilamide. It holds its shape better than the polyacrylate. It will absorb 200 times its weight in water. Polyacrilamide has another amazing property—it disappears in water. Scientists have discovered another important use for polyacrylate. Its properties—maintaining a shape, absorbing water and

Light travels at about 186,000 miles per second in a vacuum. In air it slows down a little, and in water it slows down even more. When light passes from one medium to another it is bent or *refracted* as it changes speed. That's why a pencil in a glass of water looks broken at the water's surface. Polyacrilamide becomes transparent when it is full of water. Since the water-filled plastic is mostly water, light travels through it at the same speed as it travels through ordinary water. As a result, there is no refraction at the boundary between the polymer and water, and the polymer is invisible.

invisibility in water—make it perfectly suited to be a soft contact lens.

When you have finished experimenting, let your polymers dry on paper towels. It may take a week or more, but eventually they will all return to their presoaked size.

Key Words: polyacrylate · polyacrylamide · hydrophilic

CHALLENGE LEVEL

SLICING UP LIGHT

- an adult helper
- utility knife
- empty film canister
- ruler
- hammer
- nail
- scissors
- 3-D Firework Laser glasses (I found them on the Internet under Firework Laser glasses.)
- transparent tape

Do all kinds of light have the same spectrum? When light strikes an edge, it is bent, or *diffracted.* That's why shadows have fuzzy boundaries as you move an object farther away from the surface on which the shadow is falling and closer to the light source. What happens to light if you shine it through a series of very narrow parallel stripes? This kind of device is called a *diffraction grating.* As light passes through a diffraction grating, the light waves are bent as they emerge on the other side. Waves so close together, coming out of the grating at different angles, interfere with each other. The result is that the light is broken up into different bands, or wavelengths, and show up as a rainbow of different colors called the *spectrum.* A diffraction grating can be used to analyze the spectra of different sources of light. Do the next experiment to find out how.

Method of Investigation

NOTE: Since you will be cutting heavy plastic, have an adult helper.

1. Build a *spectroscope,* an instrument to look at spectra. A spectroscope is a tube with a slit at one end through which light passes and a small window with a diffraction grating over it at the other. Using a utility knife, have an adult cut a slit in the bottom of the film canister. It should be about ⅝ inch long and ⅛ inch wide.

2. Use the hammer and nail to make a hole in the center of the lid. Push the nail through and wiggle it around to make a window about ¼ inch in diameter.

3. Cut out a small piece of a lens from the 3-D Firework Laser glasses to use as the diffraction grating. It should fit over the inside of the window. Hold it in place with transparent tape.

4. Hold the lid over the open end of the canister

A rainbow is a spectrum. It is made up of all the colors, which combine to form white light. A spectroscope will show you the colors that make up white light. But not all sources of light will emit the full spectrum. Some light sources, such as sodium vapor streetlights, show up as bright yellow-orange lines through the spectroscope. The analysis of light by using a spectroscope can identify elements like the sodium in the streetlight. Astronomers use a sophisticated version of a spectroscope to tell what elements are present in the stars and sun.

Light sources can be materials that are heated until they glow, like the tungsten filament in an incandescent bulb. They can be materials that become excited when electrically-charged particles strike them, like a fluorescent lightbulb. They can also be light given off by a chemical reaction, such as a flame. Some lamps glow when the gas inside them is struck by electrons. Street lamps often contain mercury or sodium vapor. A mercury vapor lamp will be yellow, green, and violet. A sodium vapor lamp will be mostly yellow. Fluorescent bulbs contain mercury vapor, but they are lined with a fluorescent material that emits white light (all the wavelengths) when struck by excited mercury atoms. "Neon" is used to describe the variety of differently colored lights used for advertising purposes. But only the red lights actually contain neon gas. The blue-violet lights contain argon and other colors are produced by lining the bulbs with differently colored fluorescent materials.

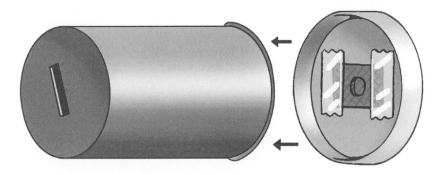

Observations & Suggestions

NOTE: Since you will be around an open flame, have an adult helper.

and direct the slit at a source of light. Look through the window at the light and rotate the lid until one of the spectra is at right angles to the slit and the spectrum is as long as possible.

5 Snap the lid on.

6 Now, use your spectroscope to look at all kinds of light sources. Incandescent bulbs, the sun (don't look directly at the sun, it can damage your eyes), streetlights, candlelight, fluorescent light, mercury vapor lights, neon lights, yellow fog lights, and cold lights (see the next experiment). Use colored pens to draw what you see and keep a record of the different spectra.

Look at the flame from a gas stove through the spectroscope. Sprinkle some salt on the flame. The yellow color you see is the typical color given off by the sodium in salt. If you look at this light through your spectroscope, you will see only bright yellow lines that are the "fingerprint" for sodium. Other elements in flames give fireworks their spectacular colors; for example, copper is bright green, calcium is orange, and strontium is red.

Key Words: diffraction grating • spectoscope

COLD LIGHT

Brightness and Duration (pg. 90) • Mixing White Light (pg. 92)

Lightsticks, glow bracelets, and glow necklaces are inexpensive fun. Their light is produced by a chemical reaction called *chemiluminescence*. The light is cold. But temperature can have an effect on it. Do an experiment and find out how.

CHALLENGE LEVEL

BRIGHTNESS AND DURATION

How can you prolong the life of a glow bracelet? Can you make it glow more brightly? See for yourself.

Method of Investigation

1. Prepare the hot and cold water baths.

2. Break the glass vial in each of the lightsticks according to the directions. Wait a few

minutes, then turn off the lights in the room. Make sure that all the lightsticks are all the same brightness before you begin.

3. Put one lightstick into the hot water and another into the ice water for about three minutes. The third should remain at room temperature.

4. Remove the lightsticks and compare their brightness.

MATERIALS AND EQUIPMENT

- a glass of hot water (about 120°F) Note: Do not use boiling water—it can melt the plastic tubing.
- a glass of ice water
- 3 lightsticks, all the same color (you can also use glow bracelets or glow necklaces)

A lightstick is a sealed plastic tube that contains a fluorescent dye mixed with an energy-releasing compound. Inside this solution, in a sealed glass tube, is some hydrogen peroxide, a very unstable compound that breaks down to release oxygen. When you break the glass vial, the three solutions mix. This starts a chemical reaction in which the hydrogen peroxide reacts with the energy-releasing compound. The released energy excites the fluorescent dye molecules. The dye molecules can only stay excited for an instant. When they return to their normal unexcited state, they release energy as the light which you see as a glow. The rate of this reaction is affected by temperature. When heat is added, the reaction goes faster and you see it as a brighter glow. Since there is a limited amount of chemical material in the lightstick, eventually it will be used up. The reaction goes so slowly in the freezer that you can store an activated lightstick for months before all the material is used up.

Observations & Suggestions

Which lightstick is the brightest? Which one do you think will glow the longest? Note the time and put two of the lightsticks in the freezer. After the one left at room temperature stops glowing, take one lightstick out of the freezer. Does the frozen lightstick glow when it returns to room temperature? After the second lightstick no longer glows, remove the third one from the freezer. Does it glow when it returns to room temperature? Put the third back in the freezer for another twenty-four hours. Remove it and check it to see if it glows. How long do you think you could store an activated lightstick in the freezer before it no longer glows? Can you design an experiment to find out?

MIXING WHITE LIGHT

MATERIALS AND EQUIPMENT

- an adult helper
- 3 lightsticks: one red, one green, and one blue
- small glass dish
- hammer
- nail
- work gloves
- a glass or jar

What happens when you mix light? White light can be broken up into a spectrum of seven colors, but to mix it you need only three colors—red, green, and blue. These three colors are known as the light primary colors (when you mix paints, which don't emit but absorb light, the three primaries are red, yellow, and blue). Have fun using lightsticks to mix your own white light.

Method of Investigation

NOTE: Since you wil be opening lightsticks, you must have an adult helper.

1. Activate the lightsticks. Notice that the blue is less intense than the green or the red.

2. Put on a pair of work gloves. Make a hole in the end of each lightstick with a nail and hammer. Keep the lightsticks, hole end up, in a glass or jar. **Note:** The material in lightsticks is nontoxic; however, it may irritate your skin or eyes, and it may stain your clothing. Please handle it carefully and dispose of it safely in a refuse container.

3. Turn the blue lightstick upside down over a small glass dish and shake out about ten drops of glowing fluid.

4. Add a few drops of green to the blue and swirl the dish to mix.

5. Add red one drop at a time, mixing by swirling between drops.

Observations & Suggestions

Try mixing just green and red and see what happens. Figure out a formula for white light using all three colors. How many drops of each color do you need to produce white light? I found that red was the strongest color so I needed less of it.

Key Words: additive primary colors · mixing light

OTHER LIGHT ESSENCES

MATERIALS AND EQUIPMENT

- lightproof room
- ultraviolet or "black" lightbulb (from a party store) and lamp
- "neon" poster board or paper
- detergent powder with "brighteners"
- glow-in-the-dark decals (from party store)
- black cloth
- flashlight
- stopwatch (optional)

What makes things glow? When light shines on certain chemicals, the chemicals emit additional light. Find out more about fluorescence and phosphorescence in the next project.

Method of Investigation

1. In a lightproof room, turn on the ultraviolet lightbulb (do not look directly at the bulb). Examine the neon paper, ordinary paper, detergent, and glow-in-the-dark materials.

2. Turn off the UV light. Do any of the materials continue to emit light?

3. Put the glow-in-the-dark objects under the black cloth. Take out one object. Shine a flashlight on it for three seconds. Turn out the light. Does it continue to glow? Compare it to a glow-in-the-dark object that was not exposed to the flashlight. Is it glowing? How long does the exposed object continue to glow?

Observations & Suggestions

Chemicals that emit visible light when struck by ultraviolet light are called *fluorescent* dyes. Neon colors, some detergents, and some white papers all contain fluorescent dyes. A fluorescent material stops emitting light as soon as the black light is shut off.

Chemicals that are excited by visible light and glow for a while after the light source has been removed are called *phosphorescent*. Expose phosphorescent decals to different amounts of light. See how long they glow afterward. There is a limit to the amount of exposure you need for the maximum amount of glow-time. The directions on one package of glow-in-the-dark materials say to expose them to thirty seconds of light. Will they glow longer if you expose

them to one minute of light?

Ever notice how your TV screen or computer monitor glows in the dark after you turn it off? That's because your television and computer screens are painted on the inside with phosphorescent dyes. You can make them glow with a flashlight. Use a television or computer that has been off for a while in a dark room. Put your hand against the screen and shine a flashlight on the screen and your hand for about two minutes. Turn off the flashlight and remove your hand. You will see the screen glow around the silhouette of your hand.

Key Words: glow in the dark · phosphorescence · fluorescence

USELESS BUT FUN

Oobleck (pg. 94) • Gak® (pg. 96) • Slime® (pg. 98)

When a scientist discovers a new material, the first problem is to identify the *properties* of that material. A list of properties gives an idea of the nature of the material, and when you know its nature you can figure out some *applications* for it. Materials engineers have the fun job of figuring out how new materials can solve old problems.

In 1941, some General Electric scientists discovered an unusual polymer while trying to synthesize rubber. It looked like chewed bubble gum but didn't stick, and it was soft, elastic, pliable, and moldable. But no matter how much they played with it, no one could find a commercial use for it. Then, in 1949, an advertising executive bought $147 worth of the stuff and hired a student to put wads of it into plastic cubes. He called it Silly Putty® and the rest, as they say, is history.

Do you have talent as an inventor? You can make your own version of Silly Putty and check out its properties. Oobleck, Gak, and Slime are similar strange polymers. Compare them to the commercially prepared stuff. Perhaps you can think of a brilliant new application for them.

OOBLECK

CHALLENGE LEVEL

Method of Investigation

1. In a pie pan, mix 1 cup of cornstarch with ½ to ¾ cup of water using your fingers. Add the water gradually. You want to create a material that will pour or drip through your fingers but will not spatter when you strike it with a hard blow. If the mixture seems too dry, add a little more water.

2. To test Oobleck for its properties do the following:

   • Pat it gently with your hand. Strike it hard with your fist.

MATERIALS AND EQUIPMENT

- pie pan
- measuring cups
- cornstarch
- water
- scissors
- knife
- small glass jar
- penny
- funnel
- balloon

- Pour it and try to cut it with scissors as you pour.

- Rub it between your fingers.

Cornstarch, like all starches, is a natural polymer—a long molecule made up of many units of a smaller molecule, in this case, sugar molecules. Cornstarch absorbs water, which becomes part of its structure. A mixture of cornstarch and water is called a *non-Newtonian fluid.* It has some of the properties of a liquid and some of a solid.

- Slice it in the pan with a knife. What happens to the Oobleck?

- Roll a small amount into a ball and leave it on the countertop. Does it retain its shape?

- Pour it into a small glass jar. Place a penny on top of it. How does it sink?

- Use a funnel to pour it into a balloon. Tie a knot in the neck of the balloon. Squeeze and stretch the balloon. Does it keep its shape? Is Oobleck stretchable?

Observations & Suggestions

This amazing stuff pours like a liquid under low stress but breaks like a solid under high stress. It looks wet but when you touch it, it becomes powdery. When you put a force on it, the material expands, pushing back on the blow. The more force you put on it, the thicker it gets.

CHALLENGE LEVEL

GAK®

Method of Investigation

NOTE: Since you will be using ammonia, have an adult helper.

1. In a paper cup, mix 1 tablespoon borax with about 1 cup of water. Stir well until completely dissolved.

2. In another cup, mix 2 tablespoons Elmer's® glue with 2 tablespoons water.

3. Mix 2 tablespoons of the borax solution with the glue solution. Stir. The Gak will collect around the spoon. Knead it to get rid of the extra water. (You can mix in a few drops of disinfectant and it won't get moldy.) Keep it in a zip plastic bag when you're not playing with it.

Compare homemade Gak with commercial Silly Putty®:

- Roll each into a ball and let it rest on a countertop. How long does it take each one to become flat?

- Apply a low stress by stretching each one slowly. What is the result?

- Apply a high stress by pulling it apart quickly. What happens?

- Roll each into a ball and drop it on the floor. Which is the better bouncer? Does a bounce give it a low stress or a high one?

- Place a ball of each material on a countertop. Press it gently. Strike it quickly with your fist. What happens?

- Place a ball of each material on a piece of

MATERIALS AND EQUIPMENT

- an adult helper
- paper cups
- measuring spoons
- borax (from laundry section of supermarket)
- measuring cup
- water
- Elmer's® glue
- disinfectant (Lysol®, for example)
- zip plastic storage bag
- Silly Putty (there are several different kinds) for comparison
- a toilet paper tube or a plastic tube of the same or smaller diameter
- sheets of printed newspaper
- comic book pages
- water-soluble ink pen
- water-insoluble ink pen
- vinegar
- household ammonia (Caution: Do not inhale the fumes.)

A carbon atom has the amazing ability of linking to itself. As a result, carbon is the basis for many polymers, including plastics and starches. Silly Putty, however, is based on silicon atoms, which form chains with oxygen atoms. Silly Putty is formed by heating a silicon-oxygen polymer with boric acid. Boron atoms replace some of the silicon atoms and weak chemical bonds form between the boric atoms on the chain. These weak bonds are easily broken when a rapid force is applied to the material. However, the bonds are not broken if a force is applied slowly. This accounts for the way gravity makes it flow slowly and a blow makes it shatter.

wood and hit the ball with a hammer. What happens?

- Stuff the Gak through a tube. How does it look when it comes out the other side?

- Flatten the Silly Putty® on different printed materials and on samples of writing with water-soluble and non-soluble pens. Pick it up. Is there print on it? Try the Gak the same way. What kinds of print does each material pick up, water-soluble or water-insoluble? (Newspaper ink is water-insoluble. Is comic book ink the same?)

- Put a dime-sized piece of Gak in a small dish. Add 1 teaspoon of vinegar and stir. What happens to the Gak?

- Add 1 teaspoon of household ammonia to the dish to neutralize the dissolved Gak. How does the recovered Gak compare to the original Gak?

Water molecules are called *polar* molecules because one part is more negatively charged and the other is more positively charged. It is called a *universal solvent* because other polar materials, like salts, will dissolve in it. The material dissolved in a solvent is called the solute. The rule for figuring out what solvent to use for a particular solute is that "like dissolves like." In other words, a polar solvent will dissolve a polar solute and a nonpolar solvent, such as turpentine, will dissolve a nonpolar solute, like oil-based paints. Silly Putty is nonpolar and Gak is polar. Do you see the difference in the kind of ink each picked up?

Observations & Suggestions

Both the Silly Putty and the Gak are examples of non-Newtonian fluids. They both are made up of long

polymers that are cross-linked to each other with weak chemical bonds. Elmer's® glue contains *polyvinyl acetate,* a carbon-based polymer. When borax is added to the glue, cross-links between the polymer chains form, which give it its gel-like consistency.

When you put the Gak in the vinegar, which is an acid, water is removed from the cross-links, breaking them, and the molecules become unconnected polymers. The material now dissolves in water. Add ammonia, an alkali, and the acid is neutralized and the cross-links are free to form again, restoring the semisolid material.

Key Words: Gak • Silly Putty

SLIME

CHALLENGE LEVEL

MATERIALS AND EQUIPMENT

- an adult helper, since you will be using the stove
- measuring spoons
- borax
- measuring cups
- water
- small saucepan
- guar gum powder (try a health food store or The Vitamin Shoppe® online)
- zip plastic bag for storage
- commercially prepared Slime (from a toy or party store)
- scissors
- toilet paper tube

Method of Investigation

NOTE: Since you will be using a stove, have an adult helper.

1. Make a borax solution by mixing 1 teaspoon of borax in 1 cup of water.

2. Put 1 cup of cold water in a saucepan. Stir in ¼ teaspoon of guar gum.

3. Heat the guar gum mixture, stirring constantly, until it boils. Remove from the heat.

4. Stir in 2 teaspoons of the borax solution. Keep stirring as the slime forms.

Guar is a bean that grows in Pakistan. Both people and cattle eat it. The powder is a flour milled from the dried bean. It absorbs so much water that very little is needed as a thickener. It is used to bind water and act as a thickener in the commercial preparation of many foods. Read labels of food products and see how many places you can find guar gum.

When cool, store the slime in a zip plastic bag.

5. Here's how you can investigate the properties of homemade slime and commercial slime.

- Pull it slowly and see how it flows and stretches. See if you can stretch it into a thin film.

- Pull it sharply. Does the slime break?

- Start pouring the slime down from its container. Then tip the container slightly upward. The slime will follow itself in an upward direction.

- What happens when you pour slime and cut it with scissors as you pour?

- Put a small piece of slime on a countertop. Smash it with your fist. Does it spatter?

- Roll a small piece into a ball. Drop it on a hard surface. Does it bounce?

- Stuff the slime through a tube. How does the diameter of the slime compare to the diameter of the tube as it emerges?

Observations & Suggestions

Guar gum is a starch that dissolves in cold water. When heated, the guar molecules absorb water, making the mixture very thick and sticky. When borax is added, cross-links form which break when a quick, hard force is applied. Under low stress, however, the cross-links remain in place, allowing the material to stretch and spread.

Key Words: guar gum · Slime

CHALLENGE LEVEL

CRYSTAL FLOWERS

MATERIALS AND EQUIPMENT

- shallow dish
- measuring spoons
- salt
- scissors
- laundry bluing (Mrs. Stewart's® is the brand that works. If you can't get it in the super-market, you can get it on the Web at www.mrsstewart.com)
- household ammonia
- a piece of charcoal briquet or a piece of cut-up sponge
- food coloring

Crystal growing kits are often found in toy stores. You can make your own, however. Home-grown crystals are so lovely, they were used as centerpieces on tables during the 1930s when the economy was so depressed people couldn't afford to buy flowers. As a result, they were called "Depression flowers."

Method of Investigation

1. In the shallow dish, mix 3 tablespoons of salt, with 3 tablespoons of water, 3 tablespoons of laundry bluing, and ½ tablespoon of ammonia.

2. Set the cut up sponges or the briquet in a shallow dish and pour the solution over it. Dot the briquet or sponge with food coloring.

3. Wait. Within two hours beautiful salt crystals will form. The white salt crystals will take on the colors of the different food dyes.

Observations & Suggestions

The delicate salt crystal flowers form as the water evaporates. The solution moves up the sponge or the briquet by capillary action (see the experiment "The Capillary Factor" on page 164). The laundry bluing contains very tiny particles of a blue powder (ferric hexacyanoferrate) that are suspended in water. As the water evaporates, each blue powder particle becomes a tiny structure for the salt crystals to grow on. The ammonia speeds up the process of evaporation.

If you want your garden to continue growing, pour new solution in every few days. Break the crust at the bottom of the dish and pour the new liquid under it.

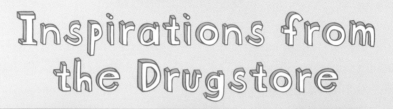

CHAPTER 4

Inspirations from the Drugstore

When you're looking for products for health or beauty, the drugstore is the answer. Apparently we think that a healthy look is beautiful. So keeping clean, feeling good, and looking "better than natural" has spawned an industry of cosmetics that can be a challenge to anyone with an inquiring mind. The term "cosmetics" has been defined by law as "articles to be rubbed, poured, sprinkled or sprayed on, introduced into, or otherwise applied to the human body or any part thereof for cleansing, beautifying, promoting attractiveness, or altering the appearance." If a cosmetic does the job it claims to do, how does it do it? Is there a difference between very expensive cosmetics and lower-priced products? What are the qualities to look for in a good face cream or nail polish? What is the science behind your skin, hair, and nails and how do cosmetics affect them? This chapter has ways to investigate.

SOAP AND DETERGENTS

Lather and Hard Water (pg. 102) • Soap vs. Detergent (pg. 103) • Deodorant Soaps (pg. 104)

Soap is made by cooking fats and oils with extremely poisonous and irritating substances such as lye, caustic soda, or potash. In order to make soap that's pleasant to use, you must have exactly the right amount of one of these irritating chemicals for the particular kind of fat you use. Too much, and the soap is grainy and strong; too little, and the soap is greasy and doesn't clean or foam well.

LATHER AND HARD WATER

CHALLENGE LEVEL

Soap bubbles form when soap molecules interact with water and make stretchable films that can hold air. But in some parts of the world, it's hard to make bubbles with local water. This so-called "hard" water contains minerals that interfere with the formation of soap films needed for suds. Water "softeners" get rid of these minerals. See for yourself in the following experiment.

MATERIALS AND EQUIPMENT

- measuring spoons
- Epsom salts
- 2 large jars with lids
- measuring cup
- distilled water
- grater
- bar of soap (Make sure the word *soap* is on the label.)
- waxed paper

Method of Investigation

1 Epsom salts (magnesium sulfate) are one mineral that makes water hard. Put 1 tablespoon of Epsom salts in one jar with a cup of distilled water.

2 Put the lid on and shake until completely dissolved.

3 Put another cup of distilled water in the other jar.

4 Grate about 2 tablespoons of soap onto some waxed paper.

5 Put ½ teaspoon of grated soap into each jar.

6 Put the lids on and shake each jar twenty times.

Observations & Suggestions

In which jar do you get suds? Will additional shaking produce suds in hard water? The white film on the top of the hard water is a reaction between minerals and soap. It's very different from the transparent soap-water film of a bubble. (Can you now explain the ring that forms around a bathtub?) Soap does not work well in hard water. So modern chemists developed a soaplike product that does. It's called detergent. Explore the differences in the next experiment.

SOAP VS. DETERGENT

CHALLENGE LEVEL

MATERIALS AND EQUIPMENT

- measuring spoons
- Epsom salts
- measuring cup
- water
- small juice glasses
- grater
- an assortment of soaps, including those listed as soap, as "bars," and as shampoos
- labels
- pen or pencil

What's the difference between a soap and a detergent?

Method of Investigation

1. Dissolve 1 tablespoon Epsom salts in 2 cups of water. This makes "hard" water.

2. Put 5 tablespoons of "hard" water in each of the glasses.

3. Put ¼ teaspoon grated soap or liquid shampoo in each glass. Use a different glass for each sample. Label each sample.

4. Cover the top of the glass with the palm of your hand and shake twenty times.

Observations & Suggestions

You should see a marked difference between the amount of foam produced by detergents and the amount produced by soaps. Detergents are not usually affected by the presence of minerals in hard water.

The amount of foam produced by a soap or detergent varies from product to product. If you would like to compare another aspect of soaps and detergents, follow the above procedure, only use distilled or "soft" tap water. It's important that you always use the same quantities of water and soap or detergent in every glass.

Another procedure for measuring the amount of foam produced by different soaps was suggested to me by a chemist at a soap company. He said that foam would form on the surface of water if you dipped a bar of soap in the water twenty times. To make the experiment fairly accurate, there are several factors, called *controls*, you will have to keep the same for all soaps.

Without controls, you can't be sure that your results are due to differences in the soaps themselves. You must use the same amount of water at the same temperature for each test. You must have the same amount of surface area for each soap sample, which means you have to use jars or bowls of the same diameter. You also must dip each soap the same number of times.

DEODORANT SOAPS

CHALLENGE LEVEL

MATERIALS AND EQUIPMENT

- an adult helper
- 1 large baking potato, peeled and washed
- pot and cover
- water
- stove
- fork
- knife
- plastic containers with lids from the supermarket deli department (about 4½ inches in diameter)
- labels
- pen or pencil
- paper towels
- regular soap
- deodorant soap

The smell of an unwashed body is due to the action of *bacteria* growing on the skin. These bacteria use sweat and *sebum*, the oily secretion of skin, as food. As bacteria multiply, an odor develops. A soap that is advertised as a deodorant soap should contain a substance that kills bacteria or retards bacterial growth. Does it really work? Experiment and find out.

Method of Investigation

NOTE: Since you will be using the stove, have an adult helper.

Note: In any experiment where you cultivate bacteria, it is important that all of your equipment be as clean as possible. The deli containers should be new or washed and dried on the upper rack of a dishwasher. Handle only the parts of your equipment that will not be touched by your experimental materials and avoid exposing your culture-growing material to the air as much as possible. If you follow these precautions, you can be reasonably certain that bacterial growth is the result of your experiment, not a contamination from the air or from unclean equipment.

1. Prepare for this experiment by working up a sweat and not bathing for twenty-four hours.

2. Put the peeled, washed, whole potato in the pot and cover with water. Boil the potato, covered, for about twenty minutes, just leaving a small crack between the cover and the pot to let the steam escape. Test for doneness by inserting a fork in the potato. If it goes through easily, the potato is done. Let the potato cool in the cooking water. This takes an hour or more.

3. Slice the cooled potato in crosswise slices about ½ inch thick. Put a slice, flat side up, in each of the four deli containers. Handle the slices as little as possible. Cover each container immediately.

SOAP

(You want to limit the exposure of the potato slices to the air.) Label the cups as follows: CONTROL, WATER, SOAP, DEODORANT SOAP.

4 Dip one of the paper towels in warm water and squeeze it so that there is some water in the towel but it is not dripping wet. Wipe one underarm once with the towel to collect your bacteria sample. Squeeze some of the water onto the potato slice marked WATER. Immediately replace the cover.

5 Rub the same towel on ordinary soap, wipe the damp underarm once, and squeeze your sample onto the slice of potato marked SOAP. Again, be sure to replace the cover as quickly as possible.

6 Take the second paper towel and prepare it as you did the first. Rub it on deodorant soap, then wipe the other underarm once. Squeeze the sample onto the potato slice marked DEODORANT, and replace its cover.

7 The control sample just has a potato slice in it. It will show you if any contamination has come from the air alone.

8 Put your experiment in a dark closet.

Observations & Suggestions

Inspect your experiment every morning and afternoon for the next few days. Bacteria colonies are tiny round circles that may be orange or shiny white. Molds are blue-green, white or black fuzzy spots. When I did this experiment, there was an obvious difference in bacterial growth. The control, which had no underarm sample, remained free of bacterial growth for three days. The deodorant soap had a spread-out orange growth, probably a yeast, but no small white colonies. The water and soap samples had many orange and white colonies.

It is clear from the results of this experiment that deodorant soaps do contain something that inhibits bacterial growth. The next question you might ask is: Does the soap kill bacteria

continued on next page ▶

on the body? Since most people wash off soap within a few seconds of putting it on their skin, the bacteria-killing substance may also wash off and not be as effective as it should be. You could check this out by washing one underarm with deodorant soap and the other with regular soap. Then repeat the procedure, keeping a control and using plain-water samples from each underarm. One would think that if the deodorant soap was effective, the underarm that was washed with it would have fewer bacteria than the underarm washed with regular soap.

How Soap Works

Chemists imagine soap molecules to have a shape like an E. Using this model, the three horizontal lines are long chains of carbon and hydrogen atoms and the vertical line is a short molecule that holds them together. During soapmaking, fats and oils are broken down as these long chains, called fatty acids, are split off. One end of a fatty acid molecule is attracted to fatty and oily substances. This is the "water hating," or *hydrophobic* end. The other end is attracted to water and is the "water loving," or *hydrophilic* end. When you wash, the water-hating end of the soap molecules sticks into the oil. The water-loving end sticks into the water. As the water moves around during the washing process, the soap molecules carry away the oil and the dirt that's in it.

Key Words: antibacterial soap · deodorant soap

A TOOTHPASTE TEST

CHALLENGE LEVEL

MATERIALS
AND
EQUIPMENT

Does brushing your teeth with toothpaste remove bacteria? Do the following experiment to find out. This experiment follows the same basic procedure as the last experiment on deodorant soap. But instead of seeing the differences between the anti-bacterial action of soap, you will be seeing the effect that brushing your teeth has on bacterial growth in your mouth.

- 1 small baking potato, peeled, washed, cooked, and sliced according to the directions on page 104
- knife
- 3 clean plastic containers and lids from the supermarket deli department (about 4½ inches in diameter)
- sterile cotton swabs
- labels
- pen or pencil
- toothbrush
- toothpaste

Method of Investigation

Plan to do this experiment just before brushing your teeth at night.

1 Place a 1/2-inch slice of cool boiled potato in each of the three deli containers. Cover to protect them from contamination from the air.

2 Wipe a dry cotton swab over one slice of potato. Re-cover immediately and label it CONTROL.

3 Wipe the back teeth of one side of your mouth three times with a new cotton swab. Wipe this swab twice over another potato slice. Cover and label this dish BEFORE.

There has been an almost endless list of *dentifrices*—substances used for cleaning teeth. These included, at one time or another: ground chalk, ground charcoal, powdered pumice stone, soap, lemon juice, ashes, tobacco mixed with honey, and a mixture of cinnamon and cream of tartar (ugh!), to name a few. In America, in 1877, William Colgate & Company, a soap company, helped usher in the age of modern toothpaste by manufacturing a dental cream. It was sold in a jar. In 1896, Colgate® wanted to add a gimmick to the product to promote it, so they put the dental cream in tubes made of tin. The instructions told customers to "press from the bottom" and a toothpaste "ribbon" would be squeezed out the other end directly onto the toothbrush. Toothpaste squeezed from a tube was a smash hit and was a major factor in encouraging at least some Americans to brush twice a day.

continued on next page ▶

4 Brush your teeth thoroughly. Take the third cotton swab and wipe the back teeth of the other side of your mouth three times. Wipe this twice over the third potato slice and label it AFTER. Be sure to expose your potato slices to the air as little as possible.

5 Put your covered deli dishes in a dark closet. Check them every day for growth.

Observations & Suggestions

Did brushing make a difference? How sterile was the cotton swab? I found that

Tooth decay is caused by bacteria that live off food trapped between teeth. When you brush your teeth, you remove the food and some of the bacteria. Modern dentifrices contain a soft, abrasive substance that works like scouring powder—gently scraping the teeth without damaging the enamel, using glycerine to give body to the mixture, a soap or detergent as a cleaning agent (obviously, one of the better-tasting ones), and a refreshing flavoring.

my CONTROL and my AFTER looked pretty much the same. They were both covered with a light brown coating that may have been a reaction of the potato surface to the air. The part of the BEFORE potato that had been smeared with the swab from my unbrushed teeth had a milky white patch. But the untouched area around it had the same brown coating.

You can use this procedure to do any number of different experiments. When does your mouth have the greatest amount of bacteria: In the morning before brushing, during the day, or in the evening? Do different brands of toothpaste have different effects on the bacteria in your mouth? Does mouthwash kill bacteria?

Key Words: dentifrices · tooth decay

LOTIONS AND CREAMS

The outside layer of skin, called the *stratum corneum*, is made up of dead skin cells. These cells are constantly being shed. But they are replaced as cells underneath move up, keeping the layer intact. The stratum corneum varies in thickness all over your body. Calluses on your feet are particularly thick stratum corneum, and your eyelid is particularly thin. But, despite differences in thickness, the amazing thing about the top layer of skin is that it is really quite thin. The average thickness of both stratum corneum and the underlying living area is only 1/250 of an inch thick.

Most of the skin problems that are treated with cosmetics take place on the stratum corneum. Cosmetics such as skin creams and lotions are basically products for cells that are dead. They cannot be "nourished" because dead cells are no longer capable of receiving nourishment.

CHALLENGE LEVEL

DEAD SKIN CELLS

MATERIALS AND EQUIPMENT

What can you do with dead skin cells to change their appearance? Here's a simple experiment:

Method of Investigation

1. Leave the pieces of callus alone for a day. They will dry out and become quite stiff.

2. Rub lotions and creams on a dried callus. Does it make a difference?

3. Soak a piece in water. Does it change in appearance?

Observations & Suggestions

You'll find that creams and lotions won't change the appearance of the callus very much after it has dried out. But you can see a dramatic change in the callus if you soak it in water. It becomes soft and easy to bend. So the most important concern of

- 2 or 3 small pieces of callus from the foot of one of your parents (DON'T CUT IT OFF YOUR OWN FOOT! Cutting off a callus requires some skill and older people have thicker calluses than young people.)
- an assortment of hand lotions and creams
- water

cosmetic creams and lotions is to keep as much water as possible in the stratum corneum.

Key Words: skin and structure · callus · stratum corneum

A BARRIER TO EVAPORATION

MATERIALS AND EQUIPMENT

- an adult helper
- 1 envelope of unflavored gelatin
- measuring cup
- spoon
- measuring spoons
- water
- cupcake cups, aluminum foil, or paper
- cookie sheet
- refrigerator
- an assortment of face creams and lotions
- labels
- pen or pencil
- petroleum jelly

Skin creams and lotions keep the stratum corneum moist by acting as a protective barrier. Much of the water in the skin is trapped in a protein called *collagen*. Collagen is one of the proteins that make up the connective tissue of the body, the material that literally holds all our tissues together. It is the single most common protein, making up almost 30% of all body protein.

Collagen molecules line up to form fibers that do not dissolve in water. Collagen fibers make up tendons and ligaments and form a network that holds skin cells in place. When collagen is heated, it breaks down to form a simpler protein, namely gelatin, that does dissolve in hot water. When a gelatin solution cools, it forms a semisolid mass, or gel. The water in gelatin is trapped by a network of gelatin molecules in much the same way as water is trapped by collagen molecules. For this reason, gelatin can act as a "model skin" to test how well different creams and lotions act as a barrier to the evaporation of water—the goal of the next experiment.

Note: This experiment takes at least four days, if not longer, so it requires patience.

Method of Investigation

NOTE: Since you will be using the stove, have an adult helper.

1. Prepare your moisture-losing "skin." Put the powdered gelatin in the measuring cup and stir in 2 tablespoons of cold water. Allow the gelatin to absorb the water. This takes a few minutes.

2. Add enough boiling water to fill to the 1-cup mark and stir. The gelatin will fully dissolve in the hot water.

3. Put 1 tablespoon of hot gelatin into each cupcake cup. You are putting in enough gelatin to make a thin, even layer on the bottom of the cup about ¼ inch deep. You should have a cupcake cup for each sample of cream and lotion, one for petroleum jelly, and one to be left alone. Let the gelatin cool for fifteen minutes.

4. Put the cups on the cookie sheet and place them in the refrigerator to set. It is important that your refrigerator shelf be level, or you won't get an even thickness to your gelatin.

5. When your gelatin skin is firm (after at least an hour and a half), you are ready to prepare your

test. Spread a ¼-teaspoon sample of each face cream or lotion on a gelatin surface. Use a different cup for each sample. Make as even a coating as possible. Label each cup to identify the sample. Leave one gelatin surface uncoated. This will be your control, as nothing prevents water from evaporating from the uncoated sample. Petroleum jelly is the most protective material you can put on skin to retard moisture loss, so it becomes your "positive control."

6 Put your samples back in the refrigerator. Let them dry for at least four days or until the gelatin in your control is a thin, flat sheet.

Observations & Suggestions

The thickness of the gelatin under each sample of cream tells you how effective the sample is in preventing water from evaporating. The gelatin that is unprotected will become a dry-feeling, thin, flat sheet. Remove each gelatin skin by slicing a strip through the center and peeling it from the cups. The thickness of the strip is a measure of how much water has evaporated. If you want to continue running the experiment, just put the cups back in the refrigerator. After a day or so, make another comparison by slicing off more strips. Be sure to compare the thickness of the gelatin at the freshly cut end, not at the end that has been exposed to

the air. Some of the creams will keep the gelatin moist and flexible. Petroleum jelly is so effective as a barrier that it is often used to coat metal tools before they are to be stored for a long time to prevent moisture in the air from coming in contact with the metal.

Of course, real skin is very complex. The gelatin film is a very simplified model of skin, doing only one thing that skin is capable of doing—namely, holding water. Scientists often create such simple models in their laboratories before they test an effect against the much more complicated realities of nature.

Key Words: collagen · barrier creams · skin and moisture

A STUDY OF LOTIONS AND CREAMS

CHALLENGE LEVEL

MATERIALS AND EQUIPMENT

- pencil and paper
- an assortment of lotions and creams including nonwashable cold cream, moisturizers, hand and body lotion, suntan creams, etc.
- a shiny metal spatula
- water
- ruler with millimeter markings (optional)
- paper towels (for cleanup)

Cosmetic creams and lotions are a particular kind of mixture known as an *emulsion*. Emulsions contain two liquid parts that don't mix, such as water and oil. Many emulsions also contain a third substance that mixes with both, called an *emulsifier*. Everyone knows that any salad dressing containing oil and vinegar has to be shaken just before it is poured. Shaking mixes the ingredients for a very short time. When you stop, the mixture soon separates into two layers with the oil on top. But if you add an emulsifier, which mixes with both oil and water, water droplets can be spread evenly through the mixture so that they don't separate out. Mayonnaise is oil and vinegar salad dressing with egg as the emulsifier. Cosmetic creams typically contain water, oil, and soap or a similar chemical as the emulsifier. They also contain many waxy materials, which act as stiffeners or thickeners.

There are two types of emulsions. In one, oil droplets are suspended in water. This type is called an oil-in-water emulsion, or O/W. The second type is the opposite—water droplets are suspended in oil, or W/O for short. The feel of a cosmetic cream depends on which substance is "enrobing" or surrounding the droplets. Oil-in-water creams are not greasy; they usually feel cool, and they "vanish" into the skin. Water-in-oil creams feel rich and somewhat oily. They sit on the skin and don't vanish.

Be a cosmetic chemist·in the next experiment and tell if a lotion or cream is W/O or O/W.

Method of Investigation

1. Make up a data sheet as shown on page 113.

2. To test to see if a cream or lotion is O/W or W/O, spread a small amount on the spatula, add a few drops of water, and try to smear the water into the cream. If the water mixes in easily, the emulsion is O/W. If the water beads up and doesn't mix in quickly, the emulsion is W/O.

3. Another way to tell if an emulsion is W/O is to rub some on your skin. If it leaves an oily film that water forms beads on, it is a W/O emulsion.

4. Test the "peak" of a cream to see how well the emulsion was formed. Dip your finger in a cream and pull it out. Is there a long peak where you pull out your finger (or on your finger) or a short one? You can measure it in millimeters, if you wish. Examine a number

DATA SHEET

Name	Product	Type of Emulsion (O/W or W/O)	Peak	Initial Feel	End Feel

of lotions and creams to get a sense of the average length of a peak. If a peak is too long or too short, it may indicate that the emulsion was not well formed.

5 Smear a patch of each sample on the back of your hand. Rub in well. As you test each one, record your impressions of the initial feeling you get and the feeling after the "dry down" (when all the water in the cream has evaporated). Record your impressions on the data sheet. Here are some words to help you: wet, greasy, tacky (sticky to the touch), talc-y (like powder), moist, silky, slippery. A word used to describe a cream that stays on the skin after the dry down is "cushion." Some creams disappear as if you never put them on. These have no cushion. Other creams are very noticeable for a long time after application. A cushion may have some "slip" to it or it may "drag." Both terms refer to the friction you feel when you massage a cream between your fingers. "Slip" means it feels easy to move, like an oil. "Drag" resists motion and may feel sticky.

Observations & Suggestions

It should be very clear from this experiment that different creams and lotions have different properties, depending on their jobs. A lotion that is to be spread all over the body usually feels more slippery than a cream that stays in a smaller area. A "vanishing" cream may have a tacky cushion. A cold cream feels greasy and leaves a greasy residue.

Key Words: cosmetic emulsions · water-in-oil · oil-in-water · cosmetic chemistry

MAKE YOUR OWN COLD CREAM

CHALLENGE LEVEL

MATERIALS AND EQUIPMENT

- an adult helper
- a postage or kitchen scale (to weigh the wax)
- 1 ounce white beeswax (for Recipe 1), bowstring wax (for Recipe 2), or paraffin wax (used for canning, found in supermarkets or housewares stores, used in Recipe 3)
- measuring cups
- mineral oil (from the pharmacy or supermarket)
- double boiler
- boiling water
- measuring spoons
- borax (from the supermarket, in the detergent section)
- spoon or whisk for stirring
- perfume (optional)
- small jars for creams (use old cold cream jars or jars that contained marinated artichoke hearts)

Cold cream is a W/O emulsion (see page 112). It can be made with beeswax that has been treated with borax. Like fats, wax also contains fatty acids. The borax reacts with these fatty acids to produce cold cream, which emulsifies the oil and water. Cold cream got its name because it feels cool when you spread it on your skin. This is because water in the cold cream is evaporating, and evaporation has a cooling effect. The cold creams you buy in stores have many different ingredients, but you can make your own simple variations at home using the recipes in this experiment.

Method of Investigation

NOTE: Since you will be using the stove, have an adult helper.

Recipe 1:

1 Put 1 ounce of white beeswax and ½ cup of mineral oil in the top of a double boiler. Heat the beeswax and mineral oil over boiling water until the wax is completely melted.

2 Put ¼ teaspoon borax in a clean, dry measuring cup. Add boiling water to make ⅓ cup. Stir. The borax should dissolve quickly.

3 Pour the hot borax solution slowly into the hot oil-wax mixture while stirring constantly. After all the borax solution has been added, take the top pan off the bottom pan and continue stirring as it cools.

4 When the mixture is warm to the touch but not hot, you may wish to add some perfume. Stir in a few drops. If you add perfume when the mixture is still hot, it will evaporate.

Recipe 2:

A smoother version of this type of cold cream contains paraffin wax.

1 Put one ounce of beeswax, ½ ounce of paraffin wax, and ⅓ cup of mineral oil in the top of a double boiler. Heat over boiling water until all the waxes are melted.

2 Put ¼ teaspoon borax and ⅓ cup water in another small saucepan. Heat until the borax is dissolved. Remove the borax solution from the heat.

Note: In this day and age it's hard to find a pure ingredient like beeswax. I happened to get some at my local hardware store, where it is sold for waxing lines on sailboats. Some craft shops sell beeswax for candle making. An excellent source is a beeswax candle. Your best chance for finding one is a specialty shop for candles, and you might also ask at some churches. I tried to make cold cream with wax products that are easily found in the hopes that they could be substituted for pure white beeswax. I tried a wax seal used by plumbers and a wax mixture sold in drugstores for removing hair. Neither worked very well. Finally, I discovered a reasonable substitute— bowstring wax for archers, found in sporting goods stores. Cold cream made with bowstring wax is not as creamy as cold cream made with pure beeswax. But you can see the emulsion form, which is what this experiment is all about. You can also try health food stores and the Internet.

3 Pour the hot oil-wax mixture into the borax solution, stirring constantly. Continue stirring as it cools. Again, you can add perfume when it is still warm but before it is too thick. Pour into jars.

Recipe 3:

Use the following recipe to make cold cream using bowstring wax:

1 Put one ounce of bowstring wax and 6½ tablespoons of mineral oil in the top of a double boiler. Heat over boiling water until the wax is melted.

2 Put 3 tablespoons of water and ¼ teaspoon of borax in another saucepan. Heat until the borax is dissolved.

Remove the borax solution from the heat.

3 Pour the hot oil-wax mixture into the borax solution, stirring constantly. Continue stirring as it cools. Again, you can add perfume when it is still warm but before it is too thick. Pour into jars.

Observations & Suggestions

The whiteness that appears when you mix in the water is the emulsion forming as the borax reacts with a fatty acid

in the beeswax. Countless tiny droplets of water are spread in the wax-oil mixture and are held in place within the emulsion. Each droplet breaks up light, forming an opaque, white substance. An emulsion doesn't have to have a white look to it. If the droplets are small enough, as in certain hair creams, the emulsion remains clear. But when you make cold cream, the droplets are relatively large, and the mixture is snow white.

Test your homemade cold cream on the back of your hand. Test it against commercial products, following the procedure in the previous experiment (page 112).

Key Words: cold cream · borax

PERFUME

CHALLENGE LEVEL

Expensive perfumes of today are a blend of between 200 and 500 different ingredients, some of them only traces. Natural ingredients from flowers and herbs are extracted by pressing leaves and petals between layers of fat. This is an expensive and labor-intensive process which produces "essential oils." Once an essential oil is in a fat, it can then be dissolved in alcohol to make perfume. The person who creates a great perfume is trained to tell the differences between hundreds of fragrances and fragrance blends. This high-paying and important job is held by someone called a "nose." Legendary noses have been known to not only tell the difference between different rose oils, but where the roses came from, when they were grown, and where the oils were processed.

The essential oils that are combined to make perfumes not only smell different from each other, but also evaporate at different rates. This means that once a perfume is exposed to the air, its smell changes as time passes. How does perfume change over time? This experiment will show you.

Method of Investigation

1. Dip the end of a strip of filter paper in your perfume sample. Write the time on the other end of the strip. Set the strip aside.

2. After ten minutes, repeat this procedure with a second strip of filter paper. Smell your two strips. Be sure and refresh your nose between sniffs by sniffing your sleeve.

3. Repeat your procedure again twenty minutes later. Compare your freshly dipped sample with the one that is now twenty minutes old and one that is thirty minutes old. Make another test one hour after you started, then three hours, or set your own time schedule.

People first began to purposefully change the smell around them when they burned pine resin and fragrant woods, like sandalwood, as incense during religious ceremonies thousands of years ago. Fragrant smoke was thought of as a way to please the gods. Incense was burned in sickrooms to mask the smells of illness and drive away the evil spirits. So it's no surprise that the word *perfume* means "through smoke" in French.

116

Observations & Suggestions

The aroma you first smell is from the oils that evaporate first. These oils are called the "top notes" of a perfume. Just after the top notes have evaporated, the aroma left behind is the "body" of the perfume. The fragrance that remains after several hours is the "dry down." This part of the perfume contains the slowest evaporating oils.

Perfume on your skin behaves differently from perfume on filter paper.

Your skin chemistry mixes with a perfume and alters the smell. Test this idea by sniffing the perfume on the filter paper and the perfume on the inside of your wrist.

Perfume on your warm skin also evaporates faster than perfume on filter paper. It evaporates fastest when placed on "pulse points" like the wrist or inside of the elbow, where the blood supply is closest to the surface. Try the time test on your skin. Compare the smells after the same time intervals with samples on

paper. Compare smells of perfume over a pulse point with perfume placed on the back of your forearm. Experts say that perfume usually lasts about four to six hours on your skin.

One problem is that your nose adjusts to the fine perfume odor as it would to any odor, pleasant or unpleasant. After a while, you think that the perfume you're wearing has disappeared. It hasn't. You can't smell it any longer, but it's still there.

Key Words: perfume making · perfume and top notes · perfume and history

SHAMPOO AND CONDITIONERS

CHALLENGE LEVEL

MATERIALS AND EQUIPMENT

- strands of untreated hair at least 3 inches long (you might ask your local hairdresser to collect some for you)
- small rubber bands
- grater
- measuring spoons
- soap
- small dishes
- water
- shampoo
- conditioner
- hair dryer (optional)
- plastic comb with fine teeth

What effects do soap, shampoo, and conditioners have on hair? Shampooing removes sweat and dirt from the scalp. It also removes the sebum, the oily secretion of skin that protects the hair, along with the dirt that sticks to it. Clean hair feels good, although without conditioners it can be very unmanageable.

Method of Investigation

1 Make four tresses out of the cut hair for testing. Take a clump of several hundred hairs. Hold them together at one end by twisting a rubber band around them and your finger so the clump looks like a ponytail. Make the rubber band as tight as possible.

2 Prepare your test solutions. Grate about a teaspoon of soap into one dish. Add enough warm water to make a soapy solution. Put 1 teaspoon of shampoo into a second dish. Add warm water and stir with your fingers.

3 Put one tress in the soap solution and two tresses into the shampoo solution. Put the fourth tress in a dish of warm water. Stir them with your finger. Then let them sit for about five minutes.

4 Rinse each tress well under warm, running water. Be careful to keep track of how each one was treated.

5 Mix about a teaspoon of conditioner and some warm water in a fifth dish. Take one of the tresses that was in shampoo and put it in the conditioner. Stir with your finger and let it sit there for five minutes. Take it out and rinse it off.

6 Let your tresses dry or blow them dry with a hair dryer.

7 When your tresses are completely dry, comb them out. Be sure to hold the rubber band end firmly when you comb.

Observations & Suggestions

Look at the differences in shininess between your hair samples. It should be obvious that hair washed with soap is the dullest. Soap leaves a film on hair. Shampoo, which contains a detergent, doesn't. An acid rinse like lemon juice will remove a soap film. See if this is true. Try dipping your soap-treated hair into a dish of lemon juice and water and rinsing again. Does it look shinier when it is dry?

Which tress combs out most easily? If your hair samples are completely dry, and if the day is not hot and humid, you should see "flyaway" as you comb. Which tress exhibits the most flyaway? Which has the least? Comb the tress that has the most flyaway. Bring the comb near the hair but don't let it touch the hair. In which direction does the hair move? Let the hair touch the comb but don't move the comb through the hair. What happens to the flyaway? Stroke the hair with your fingers. What happens to the flyaway?

Hair conditioners may contain *lanolin*—fat from sheep that is similar to sebum. This restores some of the protection against dryness that is lost by frequent shampooing. Conditioners also contain substances that make hair easier to comb and reduce the damage caused by combing out tangles. Hair conditioners also contain chemicals that are like fabric softeners and reduce the static electricity of flyaway. Do your observations confirm these facts?

Key Words: hair conditioners · lanolin · hair and flyaway

CHAPTER 5

Inspirations from the Hardware Store

Suppose you have a special job to do, like hanging a door, or putting two pieces of wood together, or making a swing, and you have no tools. Do you think you could invent something to do the job? What if you had to start from scratch and make your own glue? Would you know where to begin? And what about all those household chemicals that remove dirt, or tarnish, or wax, or paint? Do you have any idea what they are made of?

What are the unique scientific principles that enable different items from the hardware store to do their jobs? How can you create your own, at home, from scratch? Discover the answers by doing experiments. Many scientists and engineers have made a career designing products sold in hardware stores. Perhaps you'll get hooked on it and the U.S. Patent Office will hear from you. This is the beginning of your scientific hardware adventure.

TOOLS: SIMPLE MACHINES

The Claw Hammer (pg. 123) • Screws (pg. 126)

Think of tools as extensions of human hands and muscles. Hand tools, the kind of devices most people think of when they think of tools, are designed to change the shape of materials and fasten pieces together. A hammer is an extension of a fist; cutting tools extend the ability to tear material apart.

The purpose of tools is to help people do work. *Work* is one of those words that has one meaning in everyday language and another meaning for scientists. To most people, work means what you do to make money. But to a scientist, work is the movement of materials against some resistance. When you pick up a chair, you do work. The chair is being moved against the resistance of gravity.

Tools are effective because they change the proportions of force and distance to make the work easier. You do work on a tool. Your force is called the *effort.* The tool, in turn, applies your effort to some object or material—the *resistance.*

Many tools are designed to multiply your effort. When you pull out a nail, you may apply a force of ten pounds to the handle of the hammer. The hammer multiplies your effort and applies forty pounds to the nail. The tool has made you four times as strong. This increase in your effort is called the *mechanical advantage* of the tool. However, there is a trade-off here. You only get a mechanical advantage for increased force by decreasing distance. So in order to pull the nail with a strong force, the hammer pulls it a very short distance. Your hand, with the smaller effort, moves through a greater distance.

There are two parts to scientists' definition of work: *force* and *distance.* Force is usually measured in pounds or some other unit of weight. Distance, of course, is measured in either English units (feet, etc.) or metric units (meters, etc.). Work is defined as force times distance. When science makes a term mathematical, it becomes possible to see how to produce the same effect in a variety of ways. Thus you can lift 2 pounds of material 2 feet in the air, 1 pound 4 feet, or 4 pounds 1 foot, and do the same amount of work in each case. You accomplish the same amount of work by moving a lesser force through a larger distance as you do by moving a greater force through a smaller distance.

CHALLENGE LEVEL

THE CLAW HAMMER

MATERIALS AND EQUIPMENT

- safety goggles
- a claw hammer
- 3 identical four- or six-penny nails
- a block of wood a little thicker than the length of the nails

A hammer is a variation of a simple machine, called a lever. The basic lever is a rigid bar that turns on a single point called the fulcrum. The position of the fulcrum, the effort, and the force delivered to the resistance can be changed according to the use of the lever. The claw hammer is actually two tools in one. One end of the hammerhead, the claw, is a holding tool. The other end, the face, is a striking tool for driving nails into wood. The key to the effectiveness of both is the handle. Do an experiment to see how the length of the handle determines the mechanical advantage of the hammer for you.

Method of Investigation

NOTE: Wear safety goggles when using a hammer or any tool.

1 Tap the nails into the wood about 3 inches apart so that they stand without being held. Make sure that they all stick out the same distance from the wood.

2 Hold the hammer by the back of the head. Count how many strokes you need to drive one of the nails completely into the wood.

continued on next page ▶

3 Hold the hammer in the middle of the handle. Again, count the number of strokes needed to drive in the nail.

4 Finally, hold the hammer at the end of the handle. Count the number of strokes needed to drive in the third nail.

When you use a hammer to drive in a nail, the effort and the fulcrum are in the same place—your hand. The hammerhead delivers the force to the resistance. This kind of arrangement, effort and fulcrum together at one end of the lever with the resistance force at the other end, gives an increase in speed. The longer the distance between the effort-fulcrum and the resistance, the greater the speed.

There are many variations of this kind of lever. A fishing rod throws the line farther than you could throw it with your arm. A baseball bat drives the ball farther when you hold it at its end and give a full swing. When you choke up on the bat, the ball will never leave the ballpark. In fact, your arm is this kind of lever whenever you throw something. Can you now explain why it is more effective to throw with your whole arm rather than flip an object from your elbow?

Observations & Suggestions

Any carpenter will tell you that you should hold a hammer at the end of the handle when you drive in a nail. How do your results support this idea?

In which case is the hammerhead moving fastest when it strikes the nail? Where does it bounce off the nail head the highest?

Here's how a hammer works: The force delivered by the face of the head depends on two things—the weight of the hammerhead, and how fast it's moving on impact. Collision with the nail brings the motion of the hammer to a complete stop. The greater the speed on impact, the greater the force delivered to the nail. By changing the position of your hand on the handle, you change the speed of the moving head.

When you pull out a nail, the nail is held in the claws, the fulcrum is the back of the hammerhead, and the effort is your hand on the handle. So the fulcrum is between the effort and the resistance. In this kind of lever, the distance from the resistance-fulcrum to your effort determines how much your effort is multiplied. Try and

pull out a nail by holding the hammer handle up near the hammerhead. Then try by holding it near the end. You'll see that it is much easier to remove the nail when your effort is at the end of the handle.

It's easy to figure out the mechanical advantage of a lever. This will tell how much your effort is multiplied by the tool. Measure the distance from your hand to the fulcrum. This distance is called the *effort arm* of the lever. Then measure the distance from the resistance (the nail) to the fulcrum (the back of the hammerhead). This is called the *resistance*

There are other examples of levers that multiply your effort. When you use a screwdriver to open a can of paint, pry off a bottle cap or cut a hole in a can with a can opener, or open a crate with a crowbar, you use this type of lever. All of them have the same thing in common—the distance from the resistance to the fulcrum is much shorter than the distance from your effort to the fulcrum. Work (force times distance) is done at both ends, and the amount of work is equal. When your effort is moved through a larger distance, the resistance is moved through a much smaller distance with a much greater force.

arm of the lever. When you divide the effort arm by the resistance arm, you get the mechanical advantage.

The effort arm of my hammer was 11 inches. The resistance arm was 1.5 inches. Here's the formula for the mechanical advantage:

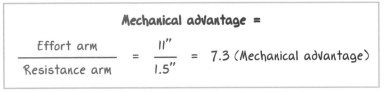

Mechanical advantage =

$$\frac{\text{Effort arm}}{\text{Resistance arm}} = \frac{11''}{1.5''} = 7.3 \text{ (Mechanical advantage)}$$

EFFORT

RESISTANCE

FULCRUM

Key Words: levers · mechanical advantage · force and distance

SCREWS

CHALLENGE LEVEL

How does a screw do its job? A screw is a ramp, or kind of wedge, wrapped around a cylinder. The surface of the ramp is the threads of a screw. Each complete turn of a screw drives it the distance between two threads.

Screws do all sorts of jobs, including holding pieces of wood together. You can also find screws at work in meat grinders, vises, and cider presses, for example. Screws have several advantages over nails. They provide more holding power because the threads increase the surface contact between the screw and the material. They can be easily removed without damaging the material, except for the hole they made. They require less force to insert.

Do an experiment to get a feel for the mechanical advantage of a screw.

Method of Investigation

1 Push a nail into the bar of soap.

2 Now screw in a screw of equal diameter. You don't need a screwdriver. Just hold the screw between your index finger and thumb, and twirl in clockwise. It will cut its way into the soap. Compare screws and nails of different diameters.

Observations & Suggestions

You can calculate the mechanical advantage of a screw. The mechanical advantage is the ratio between the circumference of the shaft of the screw and the distance between threads.

This can be expressed mathematically:

$$\frac{\text{Circumference } (\pi \times \text{diameter})}{\text{Distance between threads } (1/\text{pitch})} = \text{Mechanical advantage}$$

Screw diameters are measured by gauge number. The most common are numbers 2 through 16. Screw length is measured in inches. Nail sizes are in penny rating. The abbreviation is "d." At one time, the penny rating referred to the price you paid for nails. The abbreviation "d" comes from the word *denarius*, an early Roman coin. Today, the penny rating refers to the overall length and diameter of a nail.

The invention of the screw is credited to Archimedes, a famous Greek mathematician and inventor who lived around 250 B.C. His screw was used to raise water from rivers and streams to irrigate fields. It was made of wood and enclosed in a wooden cylinder. When the screw was turned, water climbed the "spiral staircase."

A #4 screw has a diameter of .112 inches. Its pitch is 16 threads per inch. The distance between threads is ¹/₁₆ inch or .0625 inch. Pi (π) is always 3.14. If you plug in the numbers into the formula, you get:

$$\frac{3.14 \times .112}{.0625} = 5.63 = \text{Mechanical advantage}$$

The screw multiplies your force almost six times.

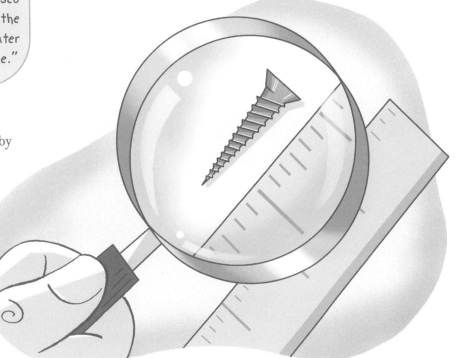

You can figure out the distance between threads by counting the number of threads in an inch, called the *pitch*. If there are sixteen threads in 1 inch, the pitch is sixteen and the distance between threads is ¹/₁₆ of an inch.

You might like to calculate the mechanical advantage for screws of other diameters. Here's a table for different screw numbers and their diameters. Figure sixteen threads per inch as the usual pitch, or .0625 inch as the distance between threads.

Screw #	1	2	3	4	5	6	7	8
Diameter	.073	.086	.099	.112	.125	.138	.151	.164

What happens to the mechanical advantage as the diameter of the screw increases?

HARD-SURFACE CLEANERS
Cleaners vs. Soaps (pg. 128) · Wetting Agents (pg. 130) · Silver Polish and Photochemistry (pg. 132)

Water is undoubtedly the cheapest and most abundant cleaner around. Unfortunately, it is not the most efficient. Although it is called the "universal solvent" because more chemicals dissolve in water than in any other liquid, there is a large class of compounds that simply don't mix at all with water—greases and oils. When dirt adheres to grease on a surface, something besides water is called for.

CLEANERS VS. SOAPS

How good are soaps and detergents for cleaning oily surfaces? When oil, water, and soap are mixed together, soap molecules organize the water and fat molecules so that they stay mixed for a while. That mixture is called an *emulsion.* Although the emulsion is often temporary, it lasts long enough to flush away the grease along with the dirt.

The cleaning solutions sold in hardware stores are called "hard-surface" soaps and detergents, as opposed to the kind of soaps used for cleaning your body and detergents used in washing clothes.

Method of Investigation
1. Put ¼ cup of cold water in each jar. Add 1 tablespoon of vegetable oil to each jar. Put the lid on one jar containing oil and water. Label this jar

CONTROL. A control has all of the elements of an experiment *except* the one you are changing.

2. Add 1 teaspoon of soap or hard-surface cleaner to each of the other jars.

MATERIALS AND EQUIPMENT
- measuring cup
- water
- small, slim olive jars with lids, as many as you can collect (Olive jars are a good substitute for test tubes. However, if you have access to test tubes, use them instead.)
- measuring spoons
- vegetable oil
- labels
- pen or pencil
- an assortment of soaps: liquid, soap flakes, detergents, etc.
- an assortment of hard-surface cleaners: Fantastik®, Mr. Clean®, Windex®, etc.
- clock with second hand

The earliest household cleaner was probably water and sand, for rubbing. Three hundred years ago, in colonial America, the main cleaners for floors and dishes were sand, strong homemade soap, and elbow grease—hard rubbing, in case you've never heard the term. Today, all hardware stores have a section for household cleaners, a baffling array of products ranging from general "all-purpose" types to specialists for polishing metals, making glass sparkle, or cleaning ovens. Instead of sand, modern cleaners contain finely ground pumice (a volcanic rock) or rottenstone. These are abrasives that, like sand, clean by rubbing off some surface along with the dirt. Harsh soaps have been replaced by a number of different chemicals: anionic surfactants, sodium citrate, calcium carbonate, and ammonia, to name a few.

Label each jar so you know which cleaner you have added.

3 Shake the jar containing oil and water five times. Using the second hand on a clock, see how long it takes to separate into two clear layers of oil and water. I found that my sample separated in about forty-five seconds.

4 Now, shake a jar containing one of your cleaning solutions five times. Measure the time it takes to separate into two layers. Repeat for each setup of oil, water, and cleaner.

Observations & Suggestions

The longer it takes for the oil and water to separate into two layers, the better the emulsifier, in this case the soap. The better the emulsion, the easier it is to rinse away dirt. I found that liquid soap was better than hard-surface cleaners. Some brands were faster than others, also. Try powdered cleaners. Dissolve a small amount in water before you add 1 teaspoonful to the oil-water mixture. Do an experiment to see how water temperature affects the emulsification.

Key Words: universal solvent · hard-surface cleaners

WETTING AGENTS

CHALLENGE LEVEL

MATERIALS AND EQUIPMENT

- scissors
- brown paper bag
- pencil
- measuring spoons
- vegetable oil
- paper towels
- a selection of hard-surface cleaners from under your sink: for general cleaning, glass, woodwork, floors, etc.
- shallow dishes
- hair dryer (optional)
- a glass of water
- straws, one for each kind of cleaner

How do hard-surface cleaners increase their wetting ability? In order for any cleaning solution to have an effect, it must come into intimate contact with the surface it is applied to. It must *wet* the surface. Water molecules wet a surface when they are more attracted to the surface molecules than they are to each other. The attraction water molecules have for each other is easiest to observe where water molecules pull together at the surface to form a kind of skin called *surface tension*. You can see surface tension as a drop forms at the end of a faucet. All liquids have surface tension, and you can easily compare different liquids by putting equal-sized drops on waxed paper and comparing the height of the drops. Some drops will be flatter than others.

Hard-surface cleaners all contain wetting agents called *surfactants*. The cleaning solutions industry has developed a variety of surfactants. Do an experiment to compare their ability as wetting agents.

Method of Investigation

1 Cut 2-inch square pieces of brown paper bag. With the pencil, label each one for a cleaning solution you intend to test. Label one CONTROL.

2 Spread about ½ teaspoon of vegetable oil on each piece of paper. The vegetable oil will sink into the paper. Spread it evenly, and wipe up any excess with paper towels.

3 Pour a sample of each cleaning solution into its own shallow dish. Dip and remove the oil-coated paper labeled for a cleaner in that solution. Let the cleaning solution dry on the paper. Use a hair dryer to speed up the drying process if you wish. After all the pieces of oiled paper have been coated with a cleaning solution and dried, you are ready to do your experiment.

4 Put a drop of water on each piece of paper. To make sure that all the drops are the same size, dip a straw into a glass of water. A small amount will remain in the end of the straw when you lift it out. Gently blow into the straw so that the drop lands on the paper.

You can compare the wetting ability of the different surfactants by the curve of the drop of water. Water will not wet an oiled surface, and a drop pulls together to create a high, rounded shape. The rounder the drop, the less the surface is getting wet. The best surfactants will cause the drop of water to spread across the paper.

Observations & Suggestions

In my experiments, I found that a window cleaner had the least wetting ability for this particular test, while a general household cleaner was the best. The water drop was the roundest on the oiled but untreated control.

You can make a survey of different hard-surface cleaners for their emulsifying ability and wetting ability. Use this procedure to measure wetting ability and the procedure on page 128 to determine emulsifying ability. Are cleaners with good surfactants also good emulsifiers? Experiment to find out.

Key Words: wetting agents · water and surface tension · surfactants

SILVER POLISH AND PHOTOCHEMISTRY

CHALLENGE LEVEL

MATERIALS AND EQUIPMENT

- water
- a piece of clean cotton cloth, about 2 inches square
- paste or cream silver polish
- a very tarnished piece of silver or silver plate
- 2 glasses
- chlorine bleach (Note: Be careful not to get this on your clothes or in a cut.)
- cone coffee filter paper or paper towel
- a funnel
- plastic wrap
- coin
- a polished flat piece of silver or silver plate
- iodine (from the drugstore)

How can light change chemicals in photography? Silver is extremely important in the development of modern photography. Images can be captured by the reaction of certain silver compounds with light. Use silver polish to get some photochemical reactions.

Method of Investigation

1. Moisten the cloth and use a small amount of silver polish to rub the tarnish off the piece of silver. The cloth should get quite black. You have now moved the silver sulfide (which is the technical name for silver tarnish) onto the cloth.

2. In a dimly lit area, put the cloth into one of the glasses and pour just enough bleach over it to cover it completely. Stir it so that the black tarnish goes into the liquid and the liquid becomes a cloudy, gray solution. You have just made silver sulfide react with the chlorine to form silver chloride—a photochemical substance.

3. Place an open cone filter into the funnel. (If you're using a paper towel, fold the paper towel in half and then in half again so that you can open it into a cone, as shown in the illustration below. Put your paper towel cone into the funnel.) Put the end of the funnel in the

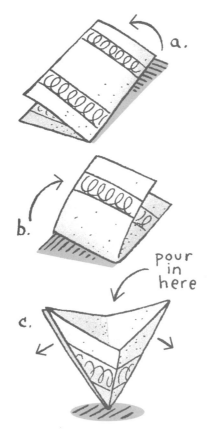

a.

b.

pour in here

c.

empty glass, and pour the silver chloride mixture into the paper cone. After the liquid has finished dripping, cut or unfold the paper cone carefully. The silver chloride has formed a thin film on the paper. Cover the paper with clear plastic wrap. You don't want it to dry out too quickly. This is your film.

4. Uncover a part of your film, put a coin on it, and

132

place it in direct sunlight. After about twenty minutes, lift the coin to see if you can see its light silhouette against the darker background.

5 Early photographers used plates of silver that had been treated chemically to form light-sensitive surfaces. You can do the same in another experiment.

In dim light, flood the surface of a polished flat piece of silver with iodine. Rinse with water. While it is wet, cover a small part with a coin and place it in a strong light. You should get a silhouette within a few minutes.

Observations & Suggestions

In both cases, you'll notice that although you'll get an image, it fades very quickly when the area that was covered is exposed to light. Also, the light-sensitive chemicals must be wet in order to react. Early photographers used "wet plates," which were really silver plates that were treated chemically and were light-sensitive when they were wet. Photography really got off the ground when images recorded on wet plates were treated with chemical "fixatives" that prevented them from darkening.

You can easily restore the silver to its previous luster with silver polish.

The day the secret of photography was announced was a momentous one. On August 19, 1839, an overflow crowd impatiently waited for news outside the French Academy of Sciences. Inside, two scientists, Joseph Niepce and Louis Daguerre, were to make public a secret process for making permanent pictures with sunlight. For many, it was the scientific revelation of the century, and rumors flew through the restless crowd. One man said, "You use a kind of tar." Another said, "No, I'm sure it's nitric acid." Finally, a nervous little man appeared at the top steps. The crowd surged forward. "Silver, iodine, and mercury," he whispered. Those three elements and the way they were used were the beginning of modern photography.

Key Words: photography and history • photography and silver

CHALLENGE LEVEL

WAXES

MATERIALS
AND
EQUIPMENT

- an adult helper
- measuring spoons
- beeswax
- paraffin
- paste floor wax
- 6 aluminum-foil muffin cups
- a large saucepan (2 quarts)
- water
- stove
- three plastic teaspoons
- thermometer showing temperatures up to the boiling point of water (212° or 100°C)

Wax protects surfaces because water will not wet it. Put a drop of water on a piece of waxed paper. See how the drop pulls together into a ball. This shows the surface tension of the water. The drop will roll around and slide right off the wax. The stems and leaves of plants, especially in tropical climates, are waxy. Water rolls off the surface without soaking into the plant. This keeps the plant from rotting. Wax on apples does the same job and can be polished to a high gloss.

Organic chemists who study waxes make note of their different properties. They are particularly interested in the temperature at which a wax melts. This so-called melting point is one way of identifying a wax and determining how pure it is. The purer a wax, the smaller the range of temperature at which it melts.

How pure are the waxes around your house? Do an experiment to find out. This procedure measures melting points that are below the boiling point of water. You can apply it to all kinds of organic substances, including fats.

Method of Investigation

NOTE: Since you will be using the stove, have an adult helper.

1. Put 2 tablespoons of each kind of wax each in its own muffin cup. Fill the pan half full of water, and float the cups containing wax in it.

2. Put the pan over a burner on the stove. You have created a "hot-water bath," as they say in the lab. Heat the bath until all the wax in each of the cups is completely melted.

3. Working quickly, fill one of the plastic spoons with one sample of melted wax and pour it into an empty muffin cup. Move the cup around so the melted wax evenly coats the bottom. Repeat with the other two waxes, using a new spoon for each. You want to have a thin, even layer of the same amount of wax in each cup.

4 Let the three samples cool for at least fifteen minutes. Put fresh cool water in the pan. Set in your three samples floating on top. Put the pan over the burner, with the tip of the thermometer in the water to measure its temperature. Start the burner and keep it on low heat. Watch very carefully to see which wax melts first. As each sample melts, note the temperature of the water. Also note the time between when a sample starts to melt and when it is completely melted.

Observations & Suggestions

Using the same wax samples, repeat this experiment several times to make sure of your results. Make sure to let the samples cool and harden between tests. Done correctly, the complete melting of a wax occurs within a few seconds and within a few degrees of change in temperature. The paste floor wax will probably melt most slowly because it is the least pure of the three samples.

Beeswax comes from honeycombs. It is secreted by the wax glands of worker honeybees. They fashion the wax into the cell of a honeycomb with their jaws. Its melting point is 108°–118°F (42°–48°C). The main ingredient in paste floor wax is carnauba wax. It is a very hard, brittle, nonsticky wax that can be buffed to a high shine. It comes from the leaves of a Brazilian palm tree. Its melting point is 180°–187°F (82.5°–86°C). Paraffin is a by-product of the petroleum industry. It is a white, hard, dry solid without any smell or taste, and as such is well suited to being in contact with food. Melted paraffin easily permeates paper that can then be used to wrap food. A good example is waxed paper. Its melting point is 125°–165°F (40°–60°C).

Since you can use and reuse your wax samples to determine melting points by this method, you can check out other waxes around your house. What kind of wax is used around cheeses? What are candles made of? Shoe polish? Lipstick?

You can use this procedure to measure the melting points of fats, substances related to oils. Check out butter, margarine, vegetable shortening, bacon grease, etc. Make sure all your samples contain the same amount of material and refrigerate the samples to get them good and hard before you run the melting-point test.

PAINTS

Paint can be defined as a colored liquid that can be applied to a surface, where it becomes a dry film. Chemists and chemical engineers have created modern paints. They test the properties of the ingredients that make up these amazing dry films that most of us take for granted.

All paint has three basic ingredients. First, there is the coloring agent or *pigment.* Pigments, as opposed to dyes, do not dissolve in the paint. They are tiny particles of colored materials that are suspended in the liquid or *vehicle* of the paint and will be the opaque color of the paint film. (Dyes, also coloring agents, do dissolve in the vehicle and stain material. They do not remain on the surface.) The vehicle, or liquid suspending the pigment, has two other parts. One part is the *binder* that actually forms the dry film and binds the pigment to the surface. The third ingredient is the *solvent* or thinner that controls the consistency of the paint in its liquid form. It is a *fugitive substance,* one that evaporates and leaves the others behind.

PAINT FILMS

What makes a good paint? The objective of any paint engineer is to produce a high-quality paint film. A paint film is extremely thin, anywhere from .001 to .004 inch thick. To examine a paint film, you need to find a way to make a film that can be easily removed from a surface. That's what the next experiment does.

Method of Investigation

NOTE: Since you will be using paints and varnishes, do this experiment in a well-ventilated area and put down newspapers first to catch spills.

1. Clean the plastic lids. You should have one for each kind of coating. Smear a thin layer of petroleum jelly over one side of each lid. This will make it easy to lift off the dried paint film.

MATERIALS AND EQUIPMENT

- newspapers
- plastic lids from coffee or tennis-ball cans
- petroleum jelly
- paints and varnishes you have on hand, including shellac, varnish, latex paint, oil-based paint
- plastic straws
- paper towels or blotting paper
- water

Mix all your paint samples thoroughly.

(a) Dip a clean plastic straw into a paint to a depth of ½ inch. **(b)** Put your finger over the top as you lift it out of the paint can. **(c)** By lifting your finger, let the paint run out of the straw onto the center of a petroleum jelly-coated cover. Gently blow out the remaining paint in the straw. Tilt the cover back and forth to get the paint to spread in a smooth layer. Repeat this procedure for each kind of paint, trying to get the same amount for each sample.

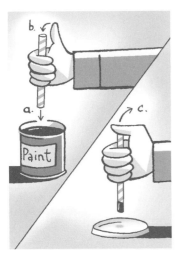

Let your samples dry overnight. The next day, peel off your paint films with a paint scraper. You may get only pieces of film, but you will be able to see differences in thickness. Pull on the films. Some kinds will be stronger than others. Fold them—some will be more flexible than others. See if the paint is waterproof. Put your largest piece of film on blotting paper or a paper towel. Put a drop of water on the paint. If the paint is not waterproof, water will seep into the blotting paper.

Observations & Suggestions

Which kind of paint dried fastest? There are three stages to drying: tacky (still wet), "tack-free" dry, and cured. Some paints take several months to become cured. Keep your paint films. See if they change over time. Which films become brittle first?

One of the properties of liquid paint is *viscosity*, or the rate at which it flows. You can compare the viscosity of paints with the following procedure: Spread newspapers to work over. Dip the end of a clean plastic straw in each sample of paint to a depth of 1 inch. Put your finger over the end of the straw and remove the sample. Work quickly in collecting your samples. Rest the straw with the end containing the paint on some object so that the paint runs downhill through the straw. Use a watch with a second hand to time how long it takes the paint to reach the bottom of the straw and run out. Different kinds of paints will have different viscosities. A low-viscosity paint will form a thinner paint film than a high-viscosity paint. Do your experiments confirm this statement?

MIX YOUR OWN PAINTS

CHALLENGE LEVEL

You can find lots of raw materials to mix your own paint in the hardware store and your home.

Method of Investigation

NOTE: Since you will be working with turpentine, do this experiment only in a well-ventilated area.

This is an open-ended experiment, where you can try all sorts of combinations to see if you can come up with a paint of your own that really works. Keep in mind that to make a paint, you need at least one binder and one pigment.

Oil-based paint

For oil-based paint, mix finely powdered pigment with a small amount of linseed oil in an aluminum-foil muffin cup. The consistency should be that of sour cream. Paint on the wooden surface and allow to dry. Clean your brush by dipping it in turpentine and wiping it clean with paper towels. Oil-based paints are the most durable. They are used for outside surfaces.

Casein paint

Artists use casein paint. Casein is milk protein. You can make your own. Mix 1 tablespoon of low-fat cottage cheese with 1 teaspoon of baking soda and 1 tablespoon of warm water. Let stand for at least one hour, stirring from time to time. The baking soda breaks down the curds into a form that dissolves. Let the mixture stand overnight. It will be ready to use as a binder when it is smooth and

clear. Mix in pigment. Add water if necessary to get the right consistency. Paint on the wood. Clean your brush with water.

Egg tempera

Egg tempera is another kind of paint artists use. Separate the white from the yolk. Ask the cook in

PIGMENTS:

- dry powdered graphite (hardware store)
- finely crushed powdered chalk
- finely crushed flower pot or terra-cotta pottery
- finely crushed charcoal
- spices such as paprika, tumeric, curry powder

BINDERS:

- linseed oil
- low-fat cottage cheese, baking soda, and water
- egg yolk beaten with water
- aluminum-foil muffin cups
- paintbrushes
- unpainted wood
- turpentine
- paper towels
- measuring spoons
- paper

your house to show you how. Beat the egg yolk with ¼ cup of water. Mix with pigment. You'll need a lot of pigment to color this paint. Try the paint on paper. Clean your brush with water. Artists use egg tempera for clear, bright color. It is very tricky to use.

Observations & Suggestions

After your paint samples have dried, rub them with your finger. See if the pigment comes loose. Mix some pigment with water alone and paint with it. After

it is dry, does the pigment stick to the surface?

Experiment with other materials as binders. Try a solution of unflavored gelatin in 3 tablespoons of water. Try white glue, liquid laundry starch, and a mixture of cornstarch and water.

Key Words: egg tempera · casein paint

ELECTRICITY

Make a Charge Detector (pg. 140) •
Make a Current Detector (pg. 143) • Batteries (pg. 146)

Electricity is a form of energy. Like light and heat and sound, electricity can be found free in nature. Giant sparks of lightning in the summer sky, your sweater sticking to your shirt, and your hair standing on end when you comb it on a cold day are all examples of *static electricity*. You can't run a television or a toaster or a lightbulb on static electricity.

   For thousands of years, static electricity was a fascinating oddity, like the lodestone, a rock that attracted metal objects that stuck to it. Then, about 275 years ago, scientists went to work on the problems of electricity and magnetism. These scientists were only interested in discovering the nature of electricity. They had no idea where their discoveries might lead. But once they discovered that electricity could move as a current through wire, inventors' imaginations caught fire. The world was electrified with countless applications.

MAKE A CHARGE DETECTOR

CHALLENGE LEVEL

An electroscope is a device that detects and measures the strength of static electricity. An electroscope has two easily charged objects, called leaves, hanging from a metal hook. When an electroscope encounters a charged object, the leaves move apart because they both pick up the same charge, and like charges repel each other. Electroscope leaves can detect both positive and negative charges. Here are directions for making several different electroscopes. You might want to try making them all and comparing them. Note: This experiment works best on a crisp, dry day.

MATERIALS AND EQUIPMENT

- metal paper clip or safety pin
- transparent tape
- a cork or piece of card-board

ELECTROSCOPE #1:
- balls of puffed rice, popcorn, or Styro-foam® packing peanuts
- silk thread

ELECTROSCOPE #2:
- flat Christmas tree tinsel

ELECTROSCOPE #3:
- tissue paper
- aluminum paint in a spray can
- scissors
- charged objects

Method of Investigation

Assemble your electroscope as follows:

1. Insulate the metal hook of the paper clip or safety pin by taping it to a cork or folded cardboard. You will hold it by the insulation.

2. *For electroscope #1:* The leaves can be two balls of puffed rice, popped popcorn, or Styrofoam® peanuts separated by 2 inches of silk thread. Hang the thread over the hook of the paper clip.

Electricity will always move toward a conductor if it gets the chance. This is the principle of the lightning rod. A piece of metal in a high place that is long enough to go into the ground will attract lightning and conduct its charge harmlessly into the ground.

For electroscope #2: Wind the middle of a piece of Christmas tree tinsel around the hook. Let the two ends hang.

For electroscope #3: Out of doors, spray some tissue paper with aluminum paint. When dry, cut a strip about ½-inch wide by 2½-inches long. Hang the middle of the strip over the hook.

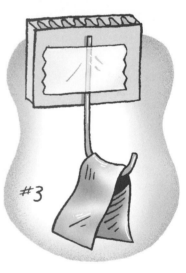

To use your electroscope:

1. Hold your electroscope by the insulating material. Bring charged objects (a rubber balloon rubbed on a sweater, a

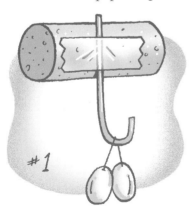

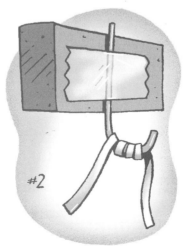

continued on next page ▶

plastic comb rubbed with wool, clothing fresh out of the dryer, glass rubbed with silk, etc.) near the leaves of your electroscope. As the charged object approaches, the leaves separate. Move your charged object away. Watch what happens to the leaves.

2 Bring your charged object near the end of the metal paper clip or safety pin that is above the insulating holder. (The end of the paper clip or pin will be the *electrode*.) Do the leaves become charged?

3 What happens when you take your charged object away from the electrode? Do the leaves stay charged?

4 What happens when you touch your charged object quickly to an electrode and then remove it?

5 What happens when you bring other charged objects near charged electroscope leaves?

Observations & Suggestions

A charged object can cause a temporary charge across a gap. This is called *induction*. You induce a charge when you bring a charged object near, but not touching, the electroscope leaves or electrode. As soon as you remove the influence of the charged object, the induced charge disappears.

The leaves remain open after the electrode has been touched by a charged object. The electrode grounds the object (removes some of its

If the leaves of an electroscope become charged, the charge is being *conducted* to the leaves through the metal wire. The motion of electricity through metal is called a *current*. Insulators do not conduct electricity. The electric charge stays in the nonmetal and is leaked into the air or into the ground. It loses its charge quickly when you touch it.

charge) and conducts the electricity to the leaves, which now remain apart.

Charged electroscope leaves will open farther or collapse when other charged objects approach. They open farther if the approaching charged object has the opposite charge, and collapse when it has the same charge.

You may notice that some objects have a stronger charge than others. Some electroscope leaves will retain a charge longer than others, as well. If you spray the puffed rice or popcorn of the first electroscope with aluminum paint, it may retain a charge longer.

Key Words: electroscope · static electricity

MAKE A CURRENT DETECTOR

MATERIALS AND EQUIPMENT

- scissors or utility knife
- cardboard
- an inexpensive compass
- 10 feet of bell wire (from a hardware store)
- flashlight battery

The electrons of metal atoms move very easily from one atom to another. Thus metals conduct a flow of electrons in a manner similar to water flowing through pipes. An electrical current is created when extra electrons are pushed into one end of the conductor and move toward the other end.

A device that detects an electric current is called a *galvanometer*. You can make a simple galvanometer quite easily and use it for lots of experiments.

The discovery of static electricity was the beginning of a story that led to our modern thinking about the structure of an atom. Atoms are so small that you can't observe their structure—even through a microscope. So scientific evidence from radioactive elements, from cloud chambers, from chemistry and from the study of electricity have helped scientists create a model of the atom.

As small as an atom is, it is made of even smaller particles that are arranged around one another like a miniature solar system. An atom has a nucleus, like the sun, that bears a positive electrical charge. Tinier particles, called *electrons*, whirl about the nucleus like miniature planets. Electrons are negatively charged. Electrons are the currency of electricity. They are able to move from one atom to another. In an uncharged atom, the total negative charge due to the orbiting electrons is equal to the total positive charge of the nucleus. But when electrons move to other atoms and the distribution becomes uneven, electricity is the result. When you rub a material to create a static charge, you are rubbing electrons from one material to another. The material that gets extra electrons is now more negative and the material that loses electrons becomes positive. Grounding allows the balance to be restored, because the ground has an unlimited supply of electron donors and electron receivers.

continued on next page ▶

Method of Investigation

1 Cut the cardboard into a rectangle that can form a cradle for the compass, with the ends bent up, as shown.

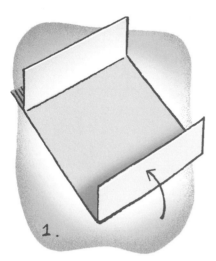

1.

2 Set the compass so that the north–south poles, as written on the dial, point to the cardboard side of the cradle.

2.

3 Hold the compass in place by winding the bell wire around the cardboard holder and compass in the same direction as the north–south compass axis. Make your coil as compact as possible. It will take about twenty-five turns. Flatten the bottom wires so the compass will rest horizontally and the needle can rotate freely. Leave both ends of wire free.

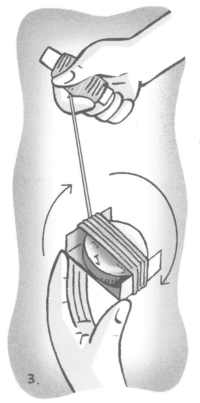

3.

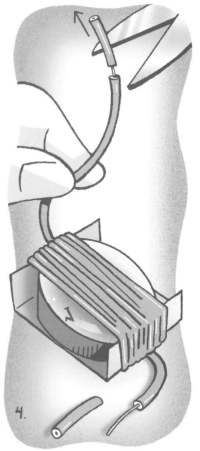

4.

4 Strip the insulation off the ends of the wires to bare about 1 inch of copper. To do this, use scissors to cut through the insulation but be careful not to cut through the wire. When the cut is complete all the way around the insulation, the insulation sleeve will pull off easily. The bare ends are the leads.

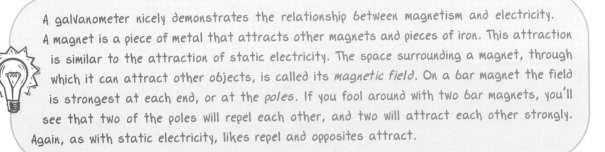

A galvanometer nicely demonstrates the relationship between magnetism and electricity. A magnet is a piece of metal that attracts other magnets and pieces of iron. This attraction is similar to the attraction of static electricity. The space surrounding a magnet, through which it can attract other objects, is called its *magnetic field*. On a bar magnet the field is strongest at each end, or at the *poles*. If you fool around with two bar magnets, you'll see that two of the poles will repel each other, and two will attract each other strongly. Again, as with static electricity, likes repel and opposites attract.

5 To use your galvanometer, set it on the table and make sure it is level so that the needle can swing freely. Turn it so that the needle hovers over the north–south axis. You won't be able to see the needle because it will be directly under the wires, but don't worry. Test your galvanometer with a flashlight battery as a source of electrical current. Put one bare wire on one electrode of the battery and the other bare wire on the opposite electrode. If the battery is not dead, the needle of the compass will move in an east–west direction. If the current is strong, the needle will spin.

Save your galvanometer for the next experiments.

Observations & Suggestions

When a current runs through a wire, it sets up a magnetic field around the wire. A coil of wire strengthens this field in your galvanometer. A current may set up a field that is stronger than the pull of the earth's poles. The compass needle now swings in an east–west direction. If the current is strong enough, the compass needle will spin rapidly.

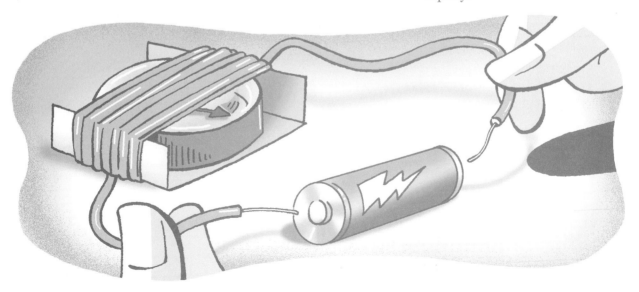

Key Words: galvanometer · current electricity

CHALLENGE LEVEL

BATTERIES

**MATERIALS
AND
EQUIPMENT**

**MATERIALS
AND
EQUIPMENT**

- scissors
- bell wire
- ruler or tape measure
- positive electrode: copper (such as a copper coupler from the plumbing section of hardware store) or carbon (such as a half of a charcoal briquet)
- negative electrode: a large galvanized nail (from a hardware store)
- electrical tape (optional)
- open-mouth pint jar
- electrolyte: white vinegar
- galvanometer (from the experiment on page 143)

A battery is a source of stored electricity. The electricity has a variety of uses. It makes an electric current through a chemical reaction. This reaction causes one electrode in the battery to lose electrons and the other to gain electrons. Electrons move from one electrode to the other, through the substance between them. This substance is called an *electrolyte*. It may be either an acid or an alkaline. In the wet cell that you make in this experiment, it will be a solution. In a dry-cell battery, the electrolyte isn't really dry. Moist, solid chemicals are used instead of a solution.

Here's how to make your own wet-cell battery:

Method of Investigation

1 Prepare your electrodes. Cut two lengths of bell wire about 8 inches long. Strip about 2 inches of insulation off one end and ½ inch off the other end of each piece. The exposed wires are your leads. Wrap the longer exposed copper wire around the center of the copper coupler or half of a briquet. Make sure there is plenty of contact between the copper or carbon and the wire. Twist the end around the wire to hold it in place. Wrap the longer lead of the other wire around the top of the galvanized nail. Put electrical tape around the connections if you wish.

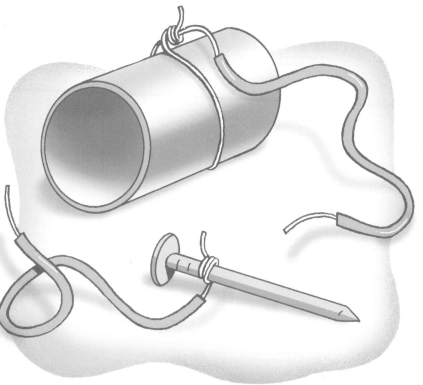

2 Fill the jar up to 1 inch below the brim with vinegar. Hang the galvanized nail electrode on one side of the jar so that it is completely submerged in the electrolyte solution, and hang the copper from the other side, so that it is completely submerged, too. They must not be touching.

3 Connect the short lead exposed from one electrode to a lead from your galvanometer. Touch the lead from the other electrode to the other lead from the galvanometer. If your battery is generating electricity, the compass needle will move from its north–south position the instant contact is made.

Observations & Suggestions

The bubbles that come out of the briquet (not the copper) are air that has been trapped during the manufacturing process. But in both cases, the tiny bubbles coming off the nail are the result of a chemical reaction. The zinc coating (put on nails so they don't rust) is reacting with the acid in vinegar and releasing tiny bubbles of hydrogen. Charged particles created in the reaction are moving through the solution from the zinc electrode to the copper electrode. When you connect the lead from the electrodes of your wet cell to the galvanometer, you are forming an electric circuit. The extra electrons that have been built up on the zinc now flow through the wire, around the coil, over the compass, and back to the copper electrode, which has a shortage of electrons. When you separate the wires so they don't make contact, you break the circuit.

See if you can generate a current with other types of electrodes and electrolytes. You may be able to get a piece of compressed

charcoal from an art-supply store. See if a lemon can serve as an electrolyte. Gently roll a lemon under your foot on the floor so the internal structure breaks down and the juice can flow more freely. Make two insertions on either side of the lemon with a slim knife. Stick a nail in one slit and the compressed charcoal in the other. Connect their leads to the galvanometer. Do you get a current? What happens if you use an alkali, like a baking-soda solution, instead of an acid? Do you get a stronger current if you add some salt to the vinegar? (A salt solution is yet another electrolyte.)

Key Words: voltaic cell · battery and definition

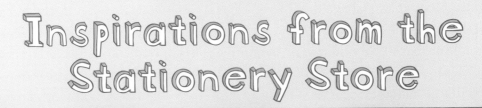

CHAPTER 6

Inspirations from the Stationery Store

Ever think about school supplies? Not just that you need to buy them from time to time, but about how they originated? Paper, pencils, pens, and paste didn't just appear, ready-made, on your desk as they exist today. Each represents a long history of human successes and failures, discoveries and inventions, based on the best scientific and technological knowledge available. In their own way, the products you buy in the stationery store represent some of the greatest technological achievements the world has ever known. What are the unique scientific properties that enable each item to do its job? How can you create your own at home? What are the basic principles of science behind each object? You can discover the answers yourself by doing your own experiments. Soon, you'll begin to appreciate your school supplies in ways you never dreamed possible.

PAPERMAKING

How would you describe paper to someone who had no idea of what it is? You might say that it's flat and thin, or that you can fold it, write on it, and burn it. But that could also describe other materials such as cardboard and fabric. There is something that all paper without exception has in common. You must do something in order to see it. Tear a piece of paper. Stroke the torn edge several times between your thumb and forefinger. Look closely at the torn edge. (A magnifying glass helps.) You'll see a fringe of tiny, threadlike fibers. Paper is a mat of millions of such tiny fibers pressed together. Tear different kinds of paper you have around the house: paper napkins, stationery, newsprint, tissues, etc. The fibers in some papers are closely knit; in others they are loosely constructed. Some paper has a filler between the fibers, some is coated, and some has a textured design. But all of the paper has tiny threads sticking out of the torn edge.

The invention of modern paper is credited to Ts'ai Lun, a Chinese nobleman, who lived about 100 A.D. He made paper from bamboo and mulberry stalks. His paper was a big improvement over the writing material available before that time. Since about 2000 B.C., people had been writing on a mat made from an Egyptian reed called *papyrus* from which we get the word *paper*. Papyrus was so thick that the best way to store it was rolled up in scrolls. Ts'ai Lun's paper was thin enough to make a pile of pages that could be written on both sides. This made books possible. Thus the first pathway of what has become the "information superhighway" was laid down.

CHALLENGE LEVEL

RECYCLED PAPER

MATERIALS AND EQUIPMENT

- 20 sheets of bathroom tissue
- egg beater or blender
- mixing bowl
- about 2 cups of water
- ½ cup liquid laundry starch
- 2-inch square of wire screening
- paper towels or newspapers
- rolling pin
- hair dryer (optional)

How is paper made? There were two problems facing early paper makers: making a flat sheet of paper, and finding a source of fibers. In the next experiment, you see how the first problem is solved. The first project is to see what paper fibers look like before they become paper. A mixture of paper fibers in water is called a *slurry*. By making paper from paper, you can see what a good paper-making slurry should look like. Then you will be better prepared to know what to look for when you experiment with other fibers.

Method of Investigation

1 Prepare the slurry. Tear the tissue into small pieces and put them in the blender or a bowl with the water. (I selected bathroom tissue because it is made to disintegrate easily in water. Most other paper has sizing added that fills up space between fibers and gives them "wet strength.") Blend or beat the mixture until it is cloudy and smooth with no big pieces. Notice the size of the fibers in the slurry. They are almost too small to see with the naked eye. Pour your slurry into the mixing bowl and add the liquid laundry starch. The starch is your sizing. Stir in additional water if necessary to make a depth of 4 inches.

2 Make a sheet of paper. This involves catching a thin, even layer of fibers

on a wire screen. Stir the slurry with your hand so that the fibers are evenly distributed. Quickly dip the wire screen into the mixture at an angle. Remove the screen horizontally so that you catch a web of slurry on the screen. It may take some practice to get an even layer of fiber on the screen. If you don't like what you've caught, turn it over on the surface of the slurry and it will go back into the mixture. People who make homemade paper call this a "kiss-off."

continued on next page ▶

3 Remove the water. Place the screen, fiber side down, on some paper towels or newspapers. Place several thicknesses of paper towels or newspapers over it. Roll it hard with a rolling pin. Gently remove the wire screen. Your sheet of newly formed paper will stick to the blotter.

4 Let your sheet of paper dry, or hurry the process by using a hair dryer. When dry, it is easy to remove the paper from the blotting material.

Observations & Suggestions

Compare your recycled paper with the original tissue. Which is more tightly meshed

Handmade paper is made in a mold with a wire screen bottom and a flat open frame, called a *deckle*, that fits over the screen. The deckle traps the slurry in a rectangular shape. After the water drains off, the deckle is removed. In handmade papers the deckle produces a tapered, ragged "deckle" edge. Some machine-made paper has an artificially produced deckle edge. You don't need a deckle to make paper if you don't care about having a straight edge.

or denser? What role does sizing play in making paper more or less dense? Hold the point of a felt-tipped pen straight down on the original tissue and your recycled paper. On which does the ink spread faster? What effect does the density of paper with sizing have on the absorption of ink? Pull apart each kind of paper. Which is stronger? Paper makers call

this difference *tensile strength*. Which paper products must have high tensile strength? Which ones should have low tensile strength?

Try making other kinds of recycled paper. Use blotting paper, art paper, and typing paper as your source of fibers. Compare your results for absorption, density, and tensile strength.

Key Words: paper making · invention of paper

LINT PAPER AND OTHER FIBERS

MATERIALS
AND
EQUIPMENT

Can you use lint from the dryer as a source of paper fibers? See for yourself.

- lint from the clothes dryer
- water
- bowl
- paper-making equipment from the last experiment (page 151)

Method of Investigation

Mix lint in water in a bowl. (A blender can help but you have to be careful that it doesn't clump around the blade. I found that a blender is not necessary.) Adjust the amount of water depending on how much lint you gather. Make paper as you did in the previous experiment (page 151).

Observations & Suggestions

Experiment with different fibers. Try marsh grass, dandelion fuzz, milkweed, corn silk, pineapple tops, cabbage, and celery. An expert in handmade paper told me that these fibers should work, although you may have to strengthen them with paper or rag fibers. She also told me that carrots don't work. Their fiber content is too low.

In my search for fibers, I chopped up absorbent cotton and cheesecloth and found that neither produced the proper slurry. I boiled sawdust and produced a huge smelly failure. I chopped up a rag and boiled it for several hours. Then I thought of using lint from the lint trap in a clothes dryer. "Eureka!" I yelled as the various colored fibers separated in a pan of water into a slightly clumpy slurry. I mixed it with my hands. My lint was multicolored because that's what had been dried. If you want white paper, clean out the lint trap and dry some white towels. In fact, the lint trap can be considered a kind of paper maker. All you have to do is figure out a way to add sizing to the flimsy layer of lint you remove from the wire screen.

Key Words: handmade paper • dryer lint

SPECIAL PROPERTIES OF PAPER

Grain (pg. 154) • Brightness (pg. 156) • Opacity (pg. 157) • Curl (pg. 158) •
Watermarks and Two-sided Characteristics (pg. 159)

What are the special properties of paper? The identifying characteristics of any material are its "properties." All materials have general properties, such as weight and volume. But it is the special properties that make one material different from all others. A good understanding of the special properties of a material does more than identify it. It can also tell you how it may be used. All paper has certain properties in common. Differences in special properties determine whether finished paper will be used for printing, wrapping, or wiping up.

GRAIN

CHALLENGE LEVEL

MATERIALS AND EQUIPMENT

- paper

Try and make a straight tear in a sheet of newspaper. When you're tearing with the grain, it's no problem. When you're tearing against the grain, it's impossible. But you don't have to try and tear paper to discover if it has a grain. Paper folds more easily with the grain than across it. Use this information to find the grain of almost any type of paper.

Method of Investigation

1. Take two identical sheets of paper. Bend one sheet in the center of the long side without creasing it. Pinch it at one end about three inches from the fold.

Machine-made paper is formed on a moving screen. This motion affects the direction in which the fibers align. More fibers line up parallel to the direction of the screen's motion than at right angles to it. This produces a grain in the paper. Since paper is more easily torn with the grain than across it, book manufacturers make sure that they stitch pages together across the grain. This way the book stays together longer.

Observations & Suggestions

Compare the size and shape of the loops you form. The paper bent with the grain will have a much flatter and narrower loop than the paper folded across the grain.

Here's how professional paper makers determine grain:

First, cut two identical strips about 4 inches long and ½ inch wide from a sheet of paper. One strip should be parallel to the long side and the other parallel to the short side. Label the strips so you know which is which.

Place the two strips side by side at the edge of a counter. Push them forward so that they hang over the edge. At some point, one strip will hang lower than the other. In this strip, the counter edge is with the grain and the bend is parallel with the grain. In the other strip, the counter edge is across the grain.

2 Do the same thing with the other sheet, only this time make your fold in a direction perpendicular to the first sheet.

BRIGHTNESS

CHALLENGE LEVEL

MATERIALS AND **EQUIPMENT**

- scissors
- ruler
- black construction paper
- tape
- different samples of uncoated white paper
- bright light

How can you compare the brightnesses of paper? Brightness is the amount of light paper reflects. Among white papers, brightness is determined by several factors: how pure the fibers are, the kinds of fillers and sizing used, and how dense the paper is. Papers that are less dense are brighter than denser papers. More porous paper is full of air pockets that reflect high amounts of light.

You can tell the difference in brightness among many kinds of papers simply by looking at them. Newsprint is clearly not as bright as typing paper. But when the difference is small, here's a way to help make the comparisons more easily.

Method of Investigation

1. Cut 1-inch-square windows in the black construction paper at least 1½ inches apart.

2. Tape a different sample of white paper under each window.

3. Shine a bright light down on the windows. The contrast with the black frame makes it easy to see differences in brightness.

Observations & Suggestions

If you compare typing papers, see if more expensive papers are brighter than cheaper papers.

Most paper used for printing reflects between 60%–90% of the light hitting its surface. When fluorescent dyes are added into coated papers, the brightness is almost 100%. The legibility of print depends on the contrast between the darkness of the ink and the brightness of the paper.

flip over

Key Words: paper and brightness

CHALLENGE LEVEL

OPACITY

MATERIALS AND EQUIPMENT

- the dark-and-white design on this page
- several kinds of paper

The degree to which a sheet of paper will prevent you from seeing through it is its *opacity*. Printers call it the "show-through" of paper and, as you can imagine, it is of great importance to printers who want to print on both sides of a sheet of paper. Paper manufacturers increase the opacity of paper by adding special mineral fillers, such as clay and talc, to the pulp and by coating finished paper with dyes.

Method of Investigation

A simple way to compare the opacity of different papers is to place them over a dark-and-white design like the one at the bottom of this page.

The design will show through some papers more than others.

Observations & Suggestions

Another method of measuring opacity is to use your black window frames from the measuring brightness experiment (page 156). Use two samples of each kind of paper.

Put a window frame around each sample. Put a sheet of white paper behind one sample and a sheet of black paper behind the other.

The black border of the windows will exaggerate the loss of brightness. You can compare this loss of brightness as a measure of opacity.

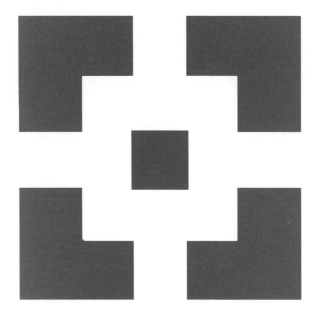

Key Words: opacity of paper • paper showthrough

CURL

CHALLENGE LEVEL

MATERIALS AND EQUIPMENT

- an adult helper
- oven
- scissors
- an assortment of different kinds of paper
- ruler
- water
- cookie sheet

What does curling tell us about paper? In this experiment, curling is a measure of how dense the paper is. The less dense the paper, the more it will curl.

Method of Investigation

NOTE: Since you will be using the stove, have an adult helper.

1. Preheat the oven to 400°F, but no higher.

2. Cut out strips of the different kinds of paper. Make them 1 inch wide by 4 inches long. They should be cut so that the grain runs across the strip. (If you are not sure which way the grain runs, do the experiment on page 154 to find out.)

3. Dip each strip of paper in water and lay it flat across the cookie sheet. Heat the strips in the oven for fifteen minutes or until dry.

Observations & Suggestions

I found that paper towels had the most curl, and blotting paper the least. Other kinds of paper were in the middle.

It is also clear that blotting paper is much more dense than paper towels.

Although paper seems pretty dry, all paper still contains a small amount of moisture. It will also absorb moisture from the air. Changes in moisture content affect the size of paper; it swells and shrinks. If more swelling occurs on one side of a sheet than other the other, the paper curls.

Key Words: paper and curl · paper and moisture

WATERMARKS AND TWO-SIDED CHARACTERISTICS

CHALLENGE LEVEL

MATERIALS AND EQUIPMENT

- several sheets of paper
- water
- cookie sheet
- pencil or ballpoint pen

atermarks are invisible designs on paper. They are made during manufacturing when the paper passes over a raised design on the dandy roller, which is the first roller to pass over the newly formed paper. The paper becomes thinner and more transparent. Thus, watermarks become visible when you hold paper up to the light or when you wet it.

When paper is dried, you can see traces of events that happened to it when it was a newly formed wet film in much the same way you can see a footprint in dried mud.

Method of Investigation

1 If you hold a sheet of paper up to the light, you can just make out the series of parallel lines that were left there by the wire screen. The fibers over the wires didn't drain quite as fast as the fibers between the wires. Thus the impression of the wires makes a pattern you can see. You can also see the marks the screen left behind in your hand made paper.

Since paper is formed on a wire screen, the underside will bear the marks of the screen. The top side, which is pressed against felt during the drying process, will have a smoother finish. See for yourself.

2 Fold over a sheet of paper and feel both sides at once with the tips of two fingers. The felt side is smoother than the wire side. If printers are only printing on one side of a sheet of paper, they prefer to print on the felt side because of its smoother finish.

3 You can make a watermark on a sheet that is already formed. Soak a sheet of paper in water until it is completely wet. Smooth the wet paper on a cookie sheet and place a dry sheet over it. Draw a design on the dry sheet with a pencil or ballpoint pen. Be careful to press hard without tearing the paper. Remove the top sheet. You'll see the impression of your watermark on the wet sheet. The design will disappear when the paper is dry (unless you hold it up to the light). But it will be easily visible if you wet the paper again.

Observations & Suggestions

There are watermarks on some fine stationery and on dollar bills.

Key Words: paper watermarks · watermarks and U.S. currency

INK

Iron Ink (pg. 160) • Artificially Aging Ink (pg. 162)

Ink has a distinct identity that no one confuses with paint or dye. Ink is defined as a liquid for making marks on a surface that will retain those marks. It is not usually used to coat surfaces, as is paint, or to color materials, as is dye. Ink can be many different colors, although the most popular shades for writing inks are blue and black. It can be applied with different kinds of writing instruments and printing presses. Most ink winds up on paper, although it can be used on other surfaces. Perhaps the single most important quality of ink is that it can stay legible for centuries, thus preserving written records of past generations. In fact, it's fair to say that without ink there might a lot less history.

IRON INK

CHALLENGE LEVEL

MATERIALS AND EQUIPMENT

- 3 or 4 iron-sulfate tablets (sold in drugstores, inexpensively, as *ferrous sulfate*, for iron-deficiency anemia)
- hot water
- funnel
- cone coffee filter paper or paper towel
- small jars with covers
- a tea bag
- a dip pen (for calligraphy writing) or a small brush

What was one of the earliest kinds of ink? Make a very black ink from a chemical reaction between a dietary supplement and tea. This kind of ink was very popular in the eighteenth and nineteenth centuries.

Method of Investigation

CAUTION: Don't drink this ink.

1. Prepare an iron-sulfate solution. If the iron-sulfate tablets have a colored coating, put them in water and stir until the coating comes off. Rinse until they're clean and let dry. Crush the tablets into a fine powder. Add about 2 teaspoons of hot water and stir. The iron sulfate will dissolve, leaving behind a chalky deposit of starch that is used to make the tablets. Pour the solution through a funnel lined with a coffee filter or a folded paper towel (see illustration on page 132). Collect the liquid iron-sulfate

solution, which is clear and colorless. Wait a few minutes and the chalky deposit will settle to the bottom. You can easily pour off the clear iron-sulfate solution.

2 Prepare the strongest tea you can make by putting ¼ cup hot water in a jar with a tea bag. Let it steep for about ten minutes before removing the tea bag.

3 Mix the two solutions together.

Observations & Suggestions

Ta da! The reaction is immediate. The mixture turns inky as tiny black particles, called a *precipitate*, form. The precipitate is called *iron tannate*. Iron tannate darkens when it is exposed to oxygen. Add a little honey to the ink to thicken it before you write with it.

You can try making ink using different sources of tannic acid and iron. See if you can make it from metallic iron.

Pour strong tea over steel wool (use the kind from the hardware store that doesn't have soap in it). Let the mixture stand overnight before you try to write with it. If it looks rusty, you've got iron oxide, instead of iron tannate. Add a little vinegar to keep the rust from forming.

There was a recipe in a very old book for an ink made by boiling iron sulfate, tea, and pomegranate peels together. If you think this might work, try it and see.

ARTIFICIALLY AGING INK

CHALLENGE LEVEL

MATERIALS AND EQUIPMENT

- household ammonia
- large jar (one that contained pickles or mayonnaise) and lid
- crow-quill pen or toothpick
- iron ink from previous experiment (page 160)
- a strip of paper ½ inch wide and 3 inches long
- rubber band

How can you age ink quickly? You don't have to wait forty years to see the aging of iron ink. You can speed up the process to less than an hour.

Method of Investigation

1. Pour just enough ammonia into the jar to cover the bottom. Screw on the lid so you don't have to smell the fumes.

2. Using the pen or toothpick, put a small dot of iron ink on the end of the strip of paper. Wait until it is completely dry before you do the next step.

3. Fold the top end of the strip so that you can hang it over the rim of the jar without letting it touch the liquid ammonia. The ink dot should be facing out so that you can easily see it through the glass. Hold the strip in place with the rubber band around the jar and screw on the lid.

Observations & Suggestions

The spot of ink first turns dark before eventually becoming completely brown. The ammonia is an alkali environment that hastens the oxidation of the iron in the ink to become rust.

Most modern writing inks do not contain iron compounds. They are mixtures of both pigments and dyes, some of which are affected by an alkaline environment. The ammonia-filled jar is a good place to see just which inks will change due to the alkali. Cut more strips of paper. Put a spot of ink from various sources on each strip, and label the source of the ink on the other end. Hang them over the ammonia by folding the top. You'll find that some inks change dramatically. However, when these strips are removed and exposed to air, the original color returns due to the evaporation of the ammonia. Once gone, the ink returns to its original state.

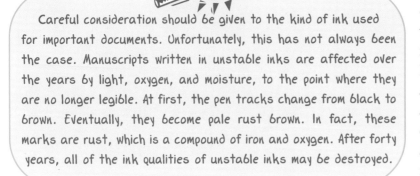

Careful consideration should be given to the kind of ink used for important documents. Unfortunately, this has not always been the case. Manuscripts written in unstable inks are affected over the years by light, oxygen, and moisture, to the point where they are no longer legible. At first, the pen tracks change from black to brown. Eventually, they become pale rust brown. In fact, these marks are rust, which is a compound of iron and oxygen. After forty years, all of the ink qualities of unstable inks may be destroyed.

Key Words: ink and permanence · manuscripts and unstable ink

WRITING INSTRUMENTS

Instruments for the Ink Pot (pg. 163) · The Capillary Factor (pg. 164) ·
Testing Chalk (pg. 166) · Make Your Own Chalk (pg. 167) · Pencils (pg. 168)

The word *pen* comes from the Latin *penna*, meaning "feather." In olden days a *penknife* was used to carve the tubular end of a goose feather or quill into the shape of a nib. For hundreds of years, writing was the job of professionals called *scribes* or *scriveners*. Putting down words was a highly skilled and time-consuming task.

CHALLENGE LEVEL

INSTRUMENTS FOR THE INK POT

MATERIALS AND EQUIPMENT

- toothpick
- ink (or food coloring)
- paper
- nail
- drinking straw (plastic or paper)
- pen nib and pen holder (try an art-supply or stationery store)
- scissors
- ruler

There are any number of devices that can put ink on paper as wavy lines. Which ones do the best job? Do an experiment and see for yourself.

Method of Investigation

1. Dip a toothpick in the ink or food coloring and draw a straight line from right to left on the piece of paper. When your hand is close to the edge of the paper, lift it up and start another line at the left-hand side of the paper. Repeat until you run out of ink.

2. Follow the same procedure using a nail.

3. Cut the straw at an angle and use it as if it were a pen to repeat the procedure.

4. Use the pen nib in a pen holder.

5. Holding each item as if it were a pen, make continuous curling loops. Try to make the loops as uniform as possible. Use a freshly cut straw, not the straw you used to make the straight line.

6. Measure the length of the lines you drew. Count the number of loops you made before you ran out of ink.

Observations & Suggestions

Which writing instrument drew the longest line? What were some of the problems of trying to draw loops with each instrument? What advantage did the straw have over the toothpick and nail? What was its biggest disadvantage?

Key Words: pen and history · quill pens

CHALLENGE LEVEL

THE CAPILLARY FACTOR

MATERIALS AND EQUIPMENT

- 3 or 4 plastic straws of different diameters (I used a 2 mm, 3 mm, and 7 mm.)
- small glass of water
- pencil
- a metric ruler showing millimeters
- blotting paper or an absorbent paper napkin
- cotton swabs
- at least one brand of bottled ink
- vegetable oil
- rubbing alcohol
- food coloring

You would not be able to put ink on paper for the purpose of writing without a little help from Mother Nature. This help comes in the force of attraction between the liquid ink and the surface of the pen and the liquid ink and the surface of the paper. The force of attraction between a liquid and a surface that allows the liquid to wet the surface is called *capillary attraction* or *capillarity*. Does the diameter of a straw affect the volume of liquid held by capillarity? Do the following experiment to find out.

Method of Investigation

NOTE: This procedure involves some fairly precise measurement. It may take several trials before you get consistent results.

1. Dip the straw with the smallest diameter several inches into the water. Slowly remove the straw and hold it up to the light. You'll see that some water remains in the end of the straw that will not drip out.

2. Do the same with the two other straws.

3. Write the diameter of each straw on your blotting paper, on the bottom of the paper about 2 inches apart.

4. Dip the narrowest straw in water. Hold it up to the light to make sure that you have trapped the liquid in the end of the straw. Carefully blot the excess water outside of the straw with a cotton swab.

5. Holding the straw vertically, put the wet end on the blotting paper above the label for that straw's diameter. Hold the straw in place, gently lifting it and touching it to the paper in the same spot until all the water is out of the straw and the blot doesn't get any larger. Outline the blot in pencil.

6. Repeat the procedure with straws of other diameters. Make sure that the blot is made only by liquid inside the straw

and that each straw is holding its maximum amount by capillarity. You may have to do several trials for each diameter.

7. Measure the diameters of the blots. Repeat the procedures using the vegetable oil, rubbing alcohol, and food coloring.

Observations & Suggestions

Amazing but true, all the blots for any particular liquid will be the same diameter! The narrow straw holds exactly as much liquid by capillarity as the wide straw. Capillarity depends on the nature of the liquid and the degree to which it wets the plastic wall of the straw. All plastic straws will attract the same volume of water regardless of diameter because they are all made of the same kind of plastic.

When you touch the end of the straw to the blotting paper the water is now more attracted to the blotting paper than to the straw so it wets the paper spreading into a circular blot. You will see a difference when you try this with ink, rubbing alcohol, and oil.

Get waxed-paper drinking straws. Compare the capillarity of a waxed-paper straw to that of a plastic straw with the same diameter.

Key Words: capillarity · pens and capillarity

TESTING CHALK

CHALLENGE LEVEL

MATERIALS AND EQUIPMENT

- white chalk
- anti-dust chalk
- waxed paper
- hammer
- 2 small glasses
- white vinegar

Chalk is a soft white mineral that is used to make white marks on blackboards. Today, there are two kinds of chalk commercially available. One is simply labeled WHITE CHALK and the other is labeled ANTI-DUST. They are different chemicals. How can you tell the difference between the two kinds of chalk? Do the acid test to see for yourself.

Method of Investigation

1. Break off a small piece of one chalk sample. Put it in a piece of waxed paper and fold the paper several times. Hammer the chalk into powder.

2. Put the powder in a glass and add a small mount of vinegar.

3. Repeat the procedure with the other chalk sample.

Observations & Suggestions

You will notice tiny bubbles rising from the anti-dust chalk. These are bubbles of carbon-dioxide gas that are released in a chemical reaction with an acid, in this case the vinegar. Anti-dust chalk is made from limestone. Its chemical name is calcium carbonate and it is known as the mineral *calcite*.

The other sample of white chalk may have a few carbon-dioxide bubbles rising from its surface due to some carbonate impurities, but there are strikingly fewer bubbles, if any. Ordinary white chalk is not limestone or "chalk" but a soft mineral called *gypsum*. Gypsum contains no carbonate and is softer than chalk.

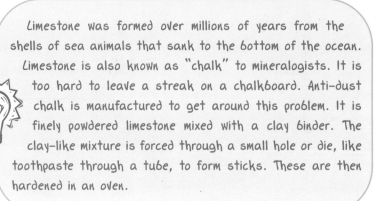

Limestone was formed over millions of years from the shells of sea animals that sank to the bottom of the ocean. Limestone is also known as "chalk" to mineralogists. It is too hard to leave a streak on a chalkboard. Anti-dust chalk is manufactured to get around this problem. It is finely powdered limestone mixed with a clay binder. The clay-like mixture is forced through a small hole or die, like toothpaste through a tube, to form sticks. These are then hardened in an oven.

Key Words: limestone and properties · gypsum and properties

CHALLENGE LEVEL

MAKE YOUR OWN CHALK

MATERIALS
AND
EQUIPMENT

- measuring spoons
- plaster of Paris (from hardware store)
- paper cups for mixing
- water
- waxed paper
- 3 eggshells
- hammer
- flour
- commercially prepared white chalk

You can make your own white chalk and anti-dust chalk.

Method of Investigation

Make ordinary chalk:

1. Mix 2 tablespoons of plaster of Paris in a paper cup with 2 tablespoons of water. The consistency should be like that of sour cream.

2. Fold a 1-foot-long piece of waxed paper in half. Pour the liquid plaster in a narrow line down the center of the waxed paper.

3. Roll the paper around the liquid plaster to form a tube. The waxed paper acts like a mold for the plaster. It takes twenty minutes for the plaster to set. Feel the plaster as it sets. It will feel warm. Let it dry for three days before you try writing with it.

Make anti-dust chalk:

1. Eggshells provide the "lime." Remove the membrane inside each of three eggshells.

2. Put the broken shells in the center of a large piece of waxed paper. Fold the paper over and over around the shells.

3. Hammer the shells to produce a fine powder. You may have to change waxed paper a few times before you get the fine powder you want.

4. Make a flour-water paste as a binder for your eggshells. Mix 1 tablespoon flour with 1 tablespoon of very hot water. Add the powdered eggshells. Shape the mixture into a stick and roll it up in a new piece of wax paper. Let it dry for three days.

Observations & Suggestions

Try out your "chalks" on a clay flowerpot. Compare them with commercially prepared chalk. Can they all be scratched with your fingernail? Do they all leave a streak on the flowerpot? Do they all erase when you rub the streak with a cloth?

Key Words: anti-dust chalk • plaster of Paris and properties

PENCILS

CHALLENGE LEVEL

MATERIALS AND EQUIPMENT

- pencil sharpener
- pencils of a range of hardnesses (I used Mongol® #1, #2, and #3.)
- metric ruler showing millimeters
- paper

The hardness of pencils is due to the addition of clay to powdered graphite in the manufacturing process. Clay is a binder for the graphite. The amount of clay is varied to make pencils of different hardnesses. How can you measure the different hardnesses of pencils? The next experiment will show you.

Method of Investigation

1. Sharpen all your pencils to points that are all the same length. Measure the length of exposed "lead" with the ruler to be sure that they are all the same length.

2. Holding the pencil vertically to the paper, make twenty lines across the page. Repeat the process with each pencil.

3. Measure the length of the worn-down tips.

Pencil Facts

- You can use a pencil to make notes in zero gravity, upside down, and underwater.

- One pencil can write 45,000 words and draw a line 35 miles long.

- More than two billion pencils are used in the United States every year.

- Almost all pencils used in the United States have erasers. Most European pencils don't.

Observations & Suggestions

The lower the number of the pencil, the softer the "lead." I found that the #1 pencil was more worn down than the #2 and #3. When I looked at the tips of the worn pencils, I could see that the softest pencil had a tip with the widest diameter; the hardest pencil had the smallest diameter; and the pencil in the middle number was worn a medium amount.

Soft pencils make the darkest marks and are most easily smudged. Hard pencils make grayer marks that are harder to smudge.

It has been suggested that old pencil marks are more difficult to erase than fresh pencil. Can you design an experiment to test this idea?

The slippery nature of graphite makes it very useful as a lubricant, especially for small, hard to reach places like locks. Rub a pencil against the teeth of a metal zipper and see if it zips more smoothly.

Pencil "lead" is not lead, a metallic element, but another element, namely carbon. Pure carbon is found in nature as crystals, as well as in noncrystalline forms such as coal. Crystals are a regular arrangement of atoms or molecules of a pure substance that have a distinct geometric shape. Carbon is an unusual element in many ways. One very unusual aspect of carbon is the difference between its two crystalline forms, graphite and diamond. In graphite crystals, carbon atoms are arranged in flat, six-atom rings that fit together like bathroom tiles. These rings form flat sheets piled on top of one another. The attraction between sheets of graphite crystals is extremely weak, so they easily slide past one another. Graphite is, therefore, very flaky and one of the softest substances on Earth. The other crystalline form of carbon, the diamond, is the hardest substance on Earth. The carbon atoms in diamonds are strongly held in a boxlike arrangement that gives the regular shape to a rough diamond crystal. The very strong attraction between all the carbon atoms in this three-dimensional structure is the cause of a diamond's extreme hardness.

ADHESIVES

Pastes, glues, gums, and pressure-sensitive tapes and labels all share one common property—they all come into very close contact with the surface of the materials, or substrates, with which they form a bond. And when I say close, I mean close. In order for an adhesive bond to form, the molecules of the adhesive must physically penetrate, actually hook into, the surface molecules of the substrate. Thus many adhesives, such as glues and pastes, start out wet and then harden into a strong film that holds the surfaces together.

TESTING GLUE FILMS

CHALLENGE LEVEL

MATERIALS AND EQUIPMENT

- jars
- plastic wrap
- rubber bands
- assortment of household glues

How do dried glues do their job? Glues form a dry film when they make an adhesive bond. You can get a good look at such films in the following experiment. Do this experiment in a well-ventilated room.

Method of Investigation

1 For each sample of glue, you'll need one jar. Stretch a square of plastic wrap across the mouth of a jar and hold it in place with a rubber band.

2 Spread a sample of glue on the plastic wrap to make a thin layer about 1 inch in diameter.

3 Let it dry.

Observations & Suggestions

How is the dry film different in appearance from the wet film? Some glues become clear when they dry. Do a test to see if the glues are waterproof. Put a drop of water on the circle of clear dry glue. If it becomes cloudy, the glue is not waterproof.

Does the glue adhere to the plastic? See if you can peel the plastic wrap away from the glue film. Glues for porous material probably will not stick. Feel the side of the film that was next to the plastic. Why is it so smooth? Does the glue adhere to metal? Repeat the test, using aluminum foil instead of plastic wrap.

Does glue shrink when it dries? If the plastic wrap wrinkles, the dried glue has shrunk.

Key Words: glues and properties

CHALLENGE LEVEL

MAKE YOUR OWN GLUE

MATERIALS AND EQUIPMENT

- an adult helper
- 2 tablespoons water
- 1 package granulated unflavored gelatin
- 1 tablespoon sugar
- small glass cup
- cooking pot
- stove
- spoon
- pot holder or tongs
- small clean paintbrush
- paper
- plastic wrap
- small jar
- rubber band

Historically, strong glue was made from the skin and hooves of animals. Such animal-hide glues had to be used when warm. When they cooled they gelled, due to the presence of an animal protein, gelatin. You can make your own version of animal glue using gelatin. It, too, must be spread when warm.

Method of Investigation

NOTE: Since you will be using the stove, have an adult helper.

1 Mix the water, gelatin, and sugar in the small glass cup. Let the mixture stand for a few minutes until all the water is mixed in. Put the cup in the pot filled with 2 inches of water.

2 Heat the mixture on the stove and stir occasionally as the water comes to a boil. Hold the cup with a pot holder or tongs. When the water starts to boil, turn off the flame. Keep the mixture over the hot water until the gelatin appears to be dissolved.

3 Use a paintbrush to try gluing some pieces of paper together. Put a sample of glue on a piece of plastic wrap stretched over a jar. Use the rubber band to hold it in place, and let it dry so you can see the film you have created. Peel off your film and examine it.

Observations & Suggestions

The sugar acts to slow down the gelling of the gelatin so that it is easier to spread. It is called a *plasticizer* by chemists. Add another tablespoon of sugar to your hot glue mixture. See if it does, in fact, take longer to set. What does a plasticizer do to the flexibility of the glue film?

This formula is not carved in stone. Experiment to see if you can improve upon it.

Key Words: glue making · animal-hide glue

A FORMULA FOR MILK GLUE

CHALLENGE LEVEL

- an adult helper
- ½ cup skim milk (you can use fresh fat-free milk or powdered milk to which you have added water)
- small frying pan
- 1 teaspoon vinegar
- spoon
- stove
- strainer
- small saucer
- 1 tablespoon warm water
- 1 teaspoon baking soda
- fork
- paper cup
- plastic wrap

Milk gets its white color from a soluble group of milk proteins called *casein*. Casein is a protein that has adhesive strength. You can use milk to make glue, but first you must separate the milk into curds and whey.

Method of Investigation

NOTE: Since you will be using the stove, have an adult helper.

1 Put the milk in the frying pan with the vinegar.

Stir constantly as you heat gently. Milk protein clots to form curds. The liquid is the whey.

2 Separate the curds and whey with the strainer.

3 Put the curds on a small saucer, add the warm water, and mash in the baking soda with a fork.

4 Force the mixture through the strainer again and store it for a day in a paper cup covered with plastic wrap.

Observations & Suggestions

When you coagulate the casein by adding acid, you produce an insoluble form of the casein. Casein cannot act as a glue in this condition, so you have to treat it to make it soluble again. You do this by neutralizing the acid by adding a base. Baking soda (sodium bicarbonate) is a base or alkali in solution. The bubbles that form when you add baking soda and water to the acid-casein curd are carbon dioxide. The

The acid in the vinegar makes the casein in the milk clump together into a solid mass. This process is similar to the coagulation of an egg when you scramble it. It is a permanent change—the casein will never again be the way it was in its natural state. You have made the soluble casein insoluble, and you have also taken the first step in cheesemaking: creating curds and whey. The coagulated casein is the curd, and the yellowish liquid is the whey.

process of getting the casein back into a soluble form takes time, so your casein glue will not be ready for at least twenty-four hours. When it is ready to use, it is a smooth milky white and creamy liquid.

Note: Commercial white glues are not casein glues. They are made from a synthetic polymer that is suspended in water. Their bond is stronger and more flexible than casein glue. Test your glue in the experiment on page 176.

Key Words: milk glue • polymers

A FORMULA FOR PASTE

CHALLENGE LEVEL

MATERIALS AND EQUIPMENT

- an adult helper
- 1 tablespoon flour
- 4 tablespoons water
- 1 teaspoon sugar
- small frying pan
- stove
- wooden spoon
- paper cup
- plastic wrap

The main ingredients in paste are starch and water. Starch is found in many plants, but its main commercial sources are seeds such as wheat, rice, and corn and tubers (storage roots) such as potatoes and arrowroot. Although these sources contain some impurities, commercial manufacturing processes produce a fairly uniform product of starch granules. Starch is a good adhesive because it is a natural polymer. Starch molecules are long chains of sugar molecules linked together. You can learn some of the peculiar properties of starch by making paste.

Method of Investigation

NOTE: Since you will be using the stove, have an adult helper.

1. Mix the flour, water, and sugar in the frying pan.

2. Gently heat the mixture, stirring constantly. When it thickens, remove it from the heat.

3. Store in a paper cup covered with plastic wrap.

Observations & Suggestions

Notice that the starch does not dissolve in cold water. It forms a suspension. When starch is heated, the starch granules swell, forming a mass called a *gel*. Different starches form gels with different properties. Make pastes substituting corn starch, potato starch, and rice starch (from health food stores) for flour. Use the paste for the four strength tests on page 176. Some of the pastes you make may only be useful as an adhesive while the mixture is warm.

The sugar you add in this formula is what professional chemists call a *plasticizer*; that is, it gives a flexibility to the material, making the dried film less likely to crack. Make paste with and without sugar. Spread equal amounts of both pastes on a nonporous surface like the plastic cover of a tennis ball or coffee can. See which film cracks more.

Thin pastes contain molecules that are shorter than starch molecules but are not broken down completely into sugar molecules. This intermediate size is called a *dextrin*. Many syrups contain dextrins. See if you can concoct a thin paste using dextrins and starches.

Key Words: starch paste · wheat paste · cornstarch · potato starch

CHALLENGE LEVEL

A FORMULA FOR GUM

MATERIALS AND EQUIPMENT

- an adult helper
- 1 packet unflavored gelatin
- 1 tablespoon cold water
- small bowl
- 1 tablespoon boiling water
- ½ teaspoon corn syrup
- spoon
- clean paintbrush
- different kinds of paper

The glue that is used for gummed labels comes from the bones and hides of animals. It can be spread on one surface and dried so it is ready to stick to another surface when moistened. The ability to become sticky when wet and nonsticky when dry in a reversible way is the reason this adhesive is used on envelopes, stamps, and labels. This is slightly different from the formula for gelatin glue found on page 171.

Method of Investigation

NOTE: Since you will be using the stove, have an adult helper.

1. Sprinkle the package of gelatin over 1 tablespoon of cold water in a small bowl. It will swell and soften in about ten minutes.

2. When the gelatin is soft, add the tablespoons of boiling water and the corn syrup. Stir until it is dissolved.

3. Paint the mixture on pieces of paper. Let dry.

4. To use as an adhesive, moisten the dried surfaces and stick them on other pieces of paper. You can make personal stamps, collages, gift cards, and many other things.

Observations & Suggestions

Gelatin is a protein manufactured by heating animal connective tissue, such as skin, tendons, and ligaments, with acid. It will not dissolve in cold water but will swell as it absorbs the water. It will dissolve in hot water, and when a gelatin solution cools, it traps the water in its structure, giving it a semisolid structure. Your gelatin adhesive will gel when cooled, but you can turn it back into a liquid by heating it over hot water.

See if you can improve the adhesive qualities of your gelatin glue by adding a teaspoon of vinegar (an acid) and heating it for a few minutes. Be careful not to let the water evaporate completely. Add water as needed to keep the level the same. Compare the strength of the bonds using the test in the next experiment.

Key Words: gelatin · gelatin glue

TESTING BOND STRENGTH

MATERIALS AND EQUIPMENT

- scissors
- ruler
- manila folders, 9 inches deep
- an assortment of pastes, glues, and tapes, including the adhesives you've made in the experiments on pages 171-175
- pencil

How strong does an adhesive bond have to be? Obviously it must be strong enough to do the job. The adhesive bond holding two pieces of paper together does not have to be as strong as a bond attaching a leg to a table. Adhesive bonds can be measured by adding weights until the bond breaks. In these tests, however, you use your own strength to get a general feel for how much force it takes to break an adhesive bond.

Method of Investigation

Testing Tensile Strength

Tensile strength is the force needed to break a bond by pulling in a direction at right angles to the bond.

1. To test tensile strength, cut ¼-inch strips down the 9-inch side of a manila folder through both sides of the folder. The bottom of a manila folder has one crease and one or two prefold marks that are designed to easily crease when the file folder is thick with papers.

2. Fold your strip on the prefold mark closest to the existing crease. You now have a long, skinny strip with a square U in the middle. Do the same thing with another strip.

3. Put a glue or paste sample on the outside small surface between the creases. Stick it to the same area on the other strip. Be sure to label the glue used for each bond. Allow the bond to dry thoroughly before you try testing it.

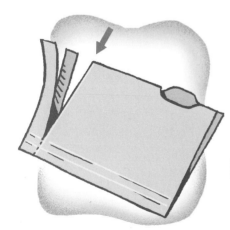

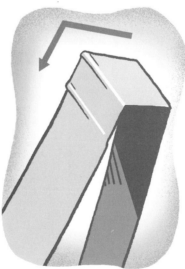

4 To test the bond, hold two strips in each hand and pull until you break the bond. Some glues will make a stronger bond than others. You should be able to feel the difference.

There are three kinds of bond failures. Look closely at the broken bond to determine the kind of failure that has occurred. *Adhesive failure* occurs when the adhesive just doesn't work. The bond never actually forms. If you use commercially prepared white glue (like Elmer's®) to adhere wood to metal, you will have adhesive failure.

Substrate failure is easy to see because the surface of the substrate has been torn. This bond doesn't separate at the place where the adhesive meets the surface. The paper fibers are ripped off the surface. Most of the bonds you'll be testing with paper adhesive break due to substrate failure.

Finally, there's *cohesive failure* of the adhesive. The separation occurs right in the middle of the adhesive film. Sometimes you'll see this when you lick a gummed envelope and it doesn't seal properly. Wallpaper paste is manufactured to have cohesive failure. You can tear wallpaper off a wall without taking any of the wall surface or leaving behind pieces of wallpaper.

Testing Shear Strength

Shear strength is the force needed to break a bond by pulling along the bond.

1 Cut two 1-inch x 8-inch strips from a manilla folder. Cut an additional 1-inch x 1½ -inch strip.

2 Fasten the short strip to a longer one with one of your pastes. Make an overlap of ⅛ inch. Write the name of the glue you used next to the bond.

3 Join the other long strip to the short one with a different adhesive.

Again, keep the overlap the same. Allow both bonds to dry thoroughly.

4 To test the bonds, grasp the two free long ends and pull your hands apart. The weaker adhesive will break first.

Testing Peel Strength

Peel strength is measured by peeling the top piece off the bottom. Use it to compare the bond strength of adhesive tapes.

continued on next page ▶

1. Put various samples of different pressure-sensitive tapes and labels on some colored paper.

2. Pull the piece of tape or label off by folding one end back and touching the surface. You can see the peel strength of the adhesive by the amount of paper fiber that comes off with it. Colored paper has more visible fibers—that's why I suggest using it for this test.

Observations & Suggestions

Pressure-sensitive tapes are made with an adhesive called an *elastomer*. Elastomers are large molecules that have rubberlike properties. You can see some of these properties with rubber cement. Put a blob of rubber cement on a nonporous surface such as the plastic top of a coffee can. Allow it to dry. The dried blob will ball up when you remove it. It can be stretched but will return to its original shape when you let go. A film of elastomers on tape or pressure-sensitive labels is very sticky and forms a weak but permanent bond.

Key Words: adhesive bond strength · elastomers

TAPES

CHALLENGE LEVEL

MATERIALS AND EQUIPMENT

- scissors
- ruler
- an assortment of tapes: masking, decorative, electrical, transparent, etc.
- blotting paper or cardboard
- metal pie pan

There are lots of different kinds of tapes in the office supply store and the hardware store. Many kinds of tape—masking tape, electrical tape, decorative tapes, tapes for sealing, reflecting tapes for bikers and joggers—all have one thing in common: They use a pressure-sensitive adhesive. Some are rubber. Others are synthetic. All of them are tacky to the touch. How do their adhesive strengths compare?

Method of Investigation

1. Cut 3-inch lengths of different tapes.

2. Press half of the length onto a piece of blotting paper or cardboard, leaving the other end free. Smooth down the adhered end to make a good, firm bond.

3. Now for the peel test. Fold back the free end of the tape so that it rests back to back with the stuck end. Peel back the adhered end, keeping the tape back to back. Some of the paper fibers will adhere to the peeled tape. The amount of paper fiber sticking to the tape is a measure of the strength of its adhesive bond.

4. Adhere half of the lengths of the different tapes to a metal pie pan. When you pull them off, you can easily feel the different adhesive strengths of the different tapes. Which did you think would be strongest? Did your tests prove your hypothesis?

Key Words: adhesive tape and peel test

RUBBER

Rubber, one of the truly important materials of modern life, got its name because of its usefulness in rubbing out pencil marks. It is elastic. It can bounce, it can stretch, and it is waterproof. These properties make rubber useful for many kinds of products from balls and tires to rainwear, as well as for glue, rubber bands, and erasers from the stationery store. Get some personal experience with its amazing properties.

CREPE RUBBER FROM RUBBER CEMENT

CHALLENGE LEVEL

MATERIALS AND EQUIPMENT

- an adult helper
- measuring spoons
- rubber cement
- a small plate

You can recover natural crepe rubber from rubber cement. Rubber cement is made by milling (mechanically rolling and kneading) many tiny pieces of crepe rubber. The milling makes the rubber as flexible as possible. The milled rubber is then mixed with highly flammable solvents.

Method of Investigation

NOTE: When you work with rubber cement, use it in a well-ventilated area and have an adult helper. Don't put a match or flame anywhere near rubber cement.

1. Spread about 2 tablespoons of rubber cement in a smooth layer on the plate.

2. Put it in a well-ventilated spot to dry. It will take at least an hour to completely dry.

3. Peel the rubber film off the plate. The rubber will stick to itself and you can roll it into a small ball. Let the ball dry, or "cure," for several days.

Observations & Suggestions

The milky-white rubber cement becomes the natural straw color of crepe rubber. The rubber ball shows many of the properties of natural rubber. If you hold it between your fingers for a while, it will become stickier due to the heat of your hand. If you squeeze it, it will spring back to its original shape. This property is called resiliency, and it is one of the most valuable properties of rubber. Resiliency gives rubber its bounce. See for yourself. Drop your little

Rubber particles in latex are suspended in water, making the sap milky-white and sticky. It is collected from rubber trees by making a small incision along the bark (known among botanists as *Hevea brasiliensis*) that is just deep enough to reach the layer inside the bark where the sap flows but is not deep enough to cut through this layer—cutting through would eventually kill the tree. A small catch cup is hung at the end of the cut, and the latex oozes out and runs down the cut to be collected at the end of the day. One mature healthy rubber tree produces about twelve pounds of rubber a year.

crepe rubber ball on the floor. It will bounce quite high. Save your little rubber ball for the erasability experiment on page 182.

Rubber is waterproof, and natural rubber was used to make rainwear. However, natural rubber was badly affected by temperature. Try painting rubber cement on a rag. Put the rubber-coated cloth in the freezer overnight. Does it get stiff? What happens when you try to wrinkle it?

You don't need to live near rubber trees to collect the sap, called latex, from plants near where you live. You can get it from dandelion and milkweed stems. Or if you live near the desert, you can get it from stubby guayule bushes. Cut the stems and gently press the milky latex out the cut end. Try to collect about a teaspoonful.

ERASABILITY

CHALLENGE LEVEL

MATERIALS AND EQUIPMENT

- pencil
- paper
- an assortment of erasers, including art gum, pencil and ink erasers, and some old erasers
- rubber bands
- balloons
- ball of rubber cement (from the previous experiment)

Compare the erasability of different kinds of rubber.

Method of Investigation

1. Make pencil marks on a sheet of paper. Try to make your lines the same darkness.

2. Try erasing the marks with the various rubber samples, erasers and other objects.

Observations & Suggestions

What happens to the surface of the erasers when you rub them against the paper? Can you rub out pencil marks with any kind of rubber? Rubber picks up as well as cuts the carbon marks of a pencil. Most erasers also contain finely ground pumice, a kind of volcanic rock, that increases the roughness of the eraser. This roughness is called an *abrasive*, which actually cuts the paper fibers at the surface. Ink erasers contain more abrasives than pencil erasers. Look closely at the surface of the paper with a magnifying glass to see how the abrasives in an eraser work.

Key Words: rubber and history · rubber and erasability

CHALLENGE LEVEL

BURNING RUBBER

MATERIALS AND EQUIPMENT

- an adult helper
- samples of rubber (a piece of rubber band, erasers)
- a small metal dish or jar cover
- matches
- aluminum foil

Rubber burns. This means that it is made up of elements that will combine with oxygen in the air. Most flammable substances are made up of two elements, hydrogen and carbon, that combine with oxygen to give off carbon dioxide and water, along with the heat and light energy of a flame.

Method of Investigation

NOTE: Since you will be using matches, have an adult helper. Do this experiment outside or in a well-ventilated area.

3 Light it with a match.

4 Hold a piece of aluminum foil about 5 inches above the flame to catch the sooty material that comes off.

—rubber sample

—aluminum foil

1 Put a small sample of rubber in a metal dish.

2 Prop it up with a small piece of aluminum foil so that the air can circulate freely around it.

Observations & Suggestions

Some rubber burns quietly, but I had a rubber band that crackled and sparked as it burned. These are tiny explosions as the hydrogen in the rubber burns. The carbon is released as sooty black smoke that you can collect. The smell of burning rubber is due to some of the chemicals added during manufacturing. Rubber manufacturers add chemicals to slow down the aging of rubber, and it is probably these chemicals that give off the characteristic bitter smell of burned rubber.

Key Words: tire burning · rubber recycling

VULCANIZED RUBBER

CHALLENGE LEVEL

- silver polish
- flat silver surface (a small silver tray or a quarter dated before 1964)
- rubber objects, like erasers, rubber bands, or balloons
- rubber cement

Most rubber has been treated with sulfur, or "vulcanized." How do you know when you have vulcanized rubber? Here's a chemical test.

Method of Investigation

1. Follow the directions on the silver polish container and polish a silver surface. Almost any silver or silver-plated object will do, as long as it has a flat area.

2. Put your rubber objects on the freshly polished surface. Paint one small part of the silver with rubber cement.

3. Leave it undisturbed for two days.

4. Look under the rubber objects for tarnish. Peel away the rubber cement.

Observations & Suggestions

Rubber that has been vulcanized contains sulfur. This experiment is a test for sulfur. Silver tarnish is a black compound called silver sulfide. All that is needed is contact between the silver and the rubber for the sulfide to form. Under which objects did tarnish form? What happened underneath the rubber cement? How can you explain your findings?

Natural crepe rubber became soft and sticky in hot weather and stiff and brittle in cold. American inventor Charles Goodyear (1800–1860) ran his family into debt trying to invent a solution to this problem. Finally, in 1830, Goodyear had a happy accident. When his wife was out of the house, and against her wishes, Goodyear mixed sulfur into some rubber. When his wife returned unexpectedly, the startled Goodyear spilled some on the stove. Much to his delight, the heated rubber was no longer sticky but firm and dry. The change was permanent but the material still had the bounce of natural rubber. Goodyear patented the process—called *Vulcanization* (After Vulcan, the Roman god of fire)—which made rubber practical for all kinds of products from tires to footwear to rubber bands. Today there are more than 50,000 applications for this material.

Key Words: Charles Goodyear • vulcanization

THE ELASTIC NATURE OF RUBBER

CHALLENGE LEVEL

MATERIALS AND EQUIPMENT

- hammer
- small nail
- wooden ruler
- thin rubber band
- pencil
- paper
- identical wire hangers

Robert Hooke (1635–1703), an English physicist, is known for the discovery of a law that defines elasticity. Rediscover Hooke's Law in the next experiment.

Method of Investigation

1. Hammer the nail into the ruler at the end of the 1-inch line.

2. Hold the ruler vertically and hang the rubber band on the nail.

3. Without stretching the rubber band, measure its length. Write down your measurement. (Remember, you must subtract the number one from your reading since you are starting at the 1-inch mark.)

4. Hang one wire hanger on the rubber band, and record its length again. Make sure that the hanger is clear of the ruler so that you are not allowing the ruler to support any of the hanger's weight.

5. Add another hanger, and record the length of the rubber band.

6. Add a third and fourth hanger, once again recording the length of the rubber band.

7. Repeat your measurements as you remove the hangers one by one.

Observations & Suggestions

How much did the rubber band stretch with each hanger? Here's what I got:

		Amount of Stretch
rubber band alone	1 $^{14}/_{16}$″	—
one hanger	2 $^{3}/_{16}$″	$^{5}/_{16}$″
two hangers	2 $^{7}/_{16}$″	$^{4}/_{16}$″
three hangers	2 $^{11}/_{16}$″	$^{4}/_{16}$″
four hangers	2 $^{15}/_{16}$″	$^{4}/_{16}$″

continued on next page ▶

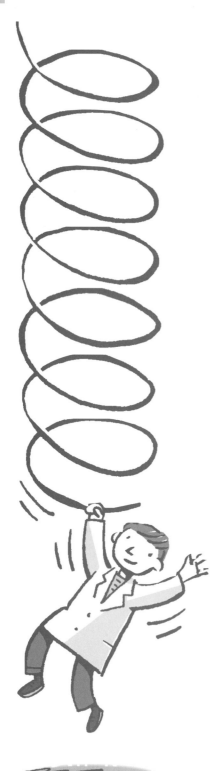

Rubber can take more of a beating than any other substance on Earth. You can stretch it, squeeze it, twist it, and bend it, and it will spring back to its original shape... usually. And you can repeat the beating, and I guarantee you will get tired before the rubber does. Rubber's ability to retain its original shape in spite of stress is called *resiliency* or *elasticity*. It's what gives a ball its bounce-back in the experiment on page 68. Other materials, such as metal and glass, are also elastic. They, too, can take certain kinds of stress and return to their original shape —but only within their elastic limits. If you bend a steel rod too far, it will stay permanently bent. Glass is even more limited, and as soon as the stress exceeds its elastic limits, it breaks.

My measurements show that for each hanger, the rubber band stretched between ⁴/₁₆ inch and ⁵/₁₆ inch. Although there is a little difference in the measurements, they are more alike than they are different. My results show Hooke's Law, which states that within the elastic limits of an elastic body, equal forces will stretch it equal amounts. We can assume that all the wire hangers weigh the same. Therefore, they will each stretch the rubber band (or elastic body) equal amounts.

Hooke's Law applies to any elastic body. including springs. (Try the experiment using a Slinky® or different-sized rubber bands.)

Key Words: Hooke's Law · rubber and elasticity

Index by Subject